Language and Adjustment Scales for the Thematic Apperception Test for Children 6-11 Years

A report on the development and standardization of objective scoring procedures for five cards of the TAT used in the Health Examination Survey of children 6-11 years of age.

U.S. DEPARTMENT OF HEALTH, EDUCATION, AND WELFARE
Public Health Service

Health Resources Administration
National Center for Health Statistics
Rockville, Md.   December 1973

NATIONAL CENTER FOR HEALTH STATISTICS

EDWARD B. PERRIN, Ph.D., *Director*

PHILIP S. LAWRENCE, Sc.D., *Deputy Director*

GAIL F. FISHER, *Assistant Director for Health Statistics Development*

WALT R. SIMMONS, M.A., *Assistant Director for Research and Scientific Development*

JOHN J. HANLON, M.D., *Medical Advisor*

JAMES E. KELLY, D.D.S., *Dental Advisor*

EDWARD E. MINTY, *Executive Officer*

ALICE HAYWOOD, *Information Officer*

DIVISION OF HEALTH EXAMINATION STATISTICS

ARTHUR J. McDOWELL, *Director*

GARRIE J. LOSEE, *Deputy Director*

HENRY W. MILLER, *Chief, Operations and Quality Control Branch*

JEAN ROBERTS, *Chief, Medical Statistics Branch*

LINCOLN I. OLIVER, *Chief, Psychological Statistics Branch*

HAROLD J. DUPUY, Ph.D., *Psychological Advisor*

COOPERATION OF THE BUREAU OF THE CENSUS

In accordance with specifications established by the National Health Survey, the Bureau of the Census, under a contractual agreement, participated in the design and selection of the sample, and carried out the first stage of the field interviewing and certain parts of the statistical processing for the Health Examination Survey.

Vital and Health Statistics-Series 2-No. 58

FOREWORD

This report summarizes research carried out under a research contract with the National Center for Health Statistics by the Institute of Behavioral Research, Texas Christian University, on the development of objectively scored cognitive and affective scales for the Thematic Apperception Test (TAT). The data for the study were obtained from story protocols given in response to the five-card, orally administered and tape-recorded version of the TAT used in the Health Examination Survey of children 6-11 years old completed in 1965. In keeping with the survey's focus on characteristics associated with growth and development, the TAT research was directed toward the construction of an objective scoring system and the formulation of scales useful in the assessment of psychological development and normal behavior.

The objectives and procedures of the present study stand in sharp contrast to the usual clinical utilization of the TAT. In typical clinical assessment practice, the TAT is administered in order to confirm hypotheses about maladjustment and personality pathology which the clinician has inferred from his knowledge of an individual's life history and from the individual's responses to other instruments, both objective and projective. In that type of use, standard scoring procedures are of little interest, and protocols are usually recorded by the clinician himself. Each clinician may use his own idiosyncratic set of notes and symbols, and his diagnosis or decision is largely a matter of subjective interpretation.

With regard to the content of the TAT scales, the approach followed in this study was based on the Center's concern in the children's survey with a broad range of developmental aspects. The research was designed to explore various aspects of psychological development, cognitive as well as emotional, which the TAT protocols might illuminate. The TAT cognitive-verbal scales identified in the analysis were more highly correlated with the cognitive criterion measures used than were the TAT affective scales with the adjustment criteria. This may reflect in part on the adjustment criteria developed. However, the relationships between attitudes expressed in fantasy and overt behavior are always indirect; a more appropriate test of validity of these personality-affective scales might be based on other personality measures as criteria.

In assessing the contribution of this TAT research, the criticism might be leveled that the objective scales are merely another measure of verbal ability. In actuality, the TAT language scales represent innovative measures of oral speech based on controlled samples of spontaneously produced speech and represent an important original contribution. That the TAT scales provide a basis for scoring verbal factors from actual samples of speech should be of considerable interest to linguistic scientists as well as to psychologists.

Janice Neman of the Institute of Behavioral Research assisted in preparing the report on this study for publication.

Arthur J. McDowell, Director
Division of Health Examination Statistics
National Center for Health Statistics

SYMBOLS	
Data not available------------------------------------	- - -
Category not applicable-------------------------------	. . .
Quantity zero---	-
Quantity more than 0 but less than 0.05-----	0.0
Figure does not meet standards of reliability or precision---------------------------	*

CONTENTS

CONTENTS—Con.

LANGUAGE AND ADJUSTMENT SCALES FOR
THE THEMATIC APPERCEPTION TEST

Ronald S. Neman, Thomas S. Brown, and S. B. Sells,
Institute of Behavioral Research, Texas Christian University

OBJECTIVES AND BACKGROUND

This report summarizes research on the development of objectively scored language and emotionality scales for a five-card, orally administered and tape-recorded version of the Thematic Apperception Test (TAT) used in the Health Examination Survey (HES) of children conducted by the National Center for Health Statistics in 1963-65. National norms for children ages 6-11 are presented for these scales.

Two studies were carried out to develop the scales and national norms. Study I[1,2] involved the development of scoring manuals, criterion measures, and TAT scales, as well as validation studies in which the TAT scales were treated as independent variables and the criteria as dependent variables. In that study major emphasis was placed on creation of usable scales. The sample of 1,224 cases employed was chosen on the basis of completeness and quality of TAT protocol from among the children examined in the first 19 of the 40 locations or "stands" in which examinations took place in the national survey.

Study II is the major focus of the present report. It was carried out on an enlarged sample which incorporated a probability subsample of the total 7,119 children examined in the second program (Cycle II) of the Health Examination Survey (appendix I). Study II involved cross-validation and refinement of the earlier study, as well as provision of national norms for the scales.

The five-card version of the TAT was administered as part of the psychological test battery included in Cycle II. That program focused on the population of noninstitutionalized children ages 6 through 11 in the United States. Since the prevalence of chronic disease in the target population of Cycle II is low, attention was directed to measurement of characteristics associated with growth and development. The total examination of each child, administered in specially designed mobile examination centers by a team of qualified professional examiners, included measures of visual and auditory acuity, anthropometric measures, dental examination, tests of respiratory function and exercise tolerance, X-rays, and other physical examination tests and procedures, as well as the psychological test battery. Details regarding the plan and operation of the survey can be found in another report.[3]

The individually administered psychological test battery included the Vocabulary and Block Design subtests of the Wechsler Intelligence Scale for Children (WISC), the Reading and Arithmetic subtests of the Wide Range Achievement Test (WRAT), and the Draw-A-Person Test (DAP) scored on the Goodenough-Harris scales, in addition to the TAT. The TAT was chosen mainly because of its potential for personality-emotionality measurement within the constraints of the survey and its requirements, while the other tests were selected primarily as intellectual-cognitive measures.

The cards included in the specially adapted version of the TAT were: card 1 (boy contemplating violin on table), card 2 (girl with books

1

beside farm family scene), card 5 (woman at doorway looking into room), card 8 BM (boy with "operation scene" in background), and card 16 (blank card). The cards were individually presented to each child, who was asked to imagine and relate a story. Responses were obtained orally, tape recorded, and later transcribed.

All cards were shown to both boys and girls, even though card 8 BM is traditionally not shown to girls.

The Cycle II battery was evaluated for the National Center for Health Statistics (NCHS) by Sells,[4] who noted with respect to the TAT: (1) that no single personality test for children known then (at the time the HES Cycle II was planned) could be recommended without qualification; (2) that because of its very general use in school and clinic, the TAT had widespread acceptance; and (3) that the planners of Cycle II believed that psychometrically acceptable scales for the TAT could be developed from the survey data, and they opted for technically sound measures in preference to the imperfect information that would be forthcoming from published self-report measures. Although other projective procedures might have been similarly used, the TAT was the method preferred.

Although inclusion of the TAT in the battery was determined mainly by interest in its relevance for measurement of affective functioning and personality, the experimental scoring manuals were prepared to measure developmental aspects of oral language as well. This recommendation by the principal investigator was accepted by the NCHS staff on the grounds that since language development data were available, they should be examined, and that such examination was congruent with one goal of the survey—the investigation of the prevalence of pathology in psychological development of American children ages 6 through 11. Within such a frame of reference, language development scales could be considered at least as relevant as personality-emotionality measures, and their inclusion in the research in addition to the thematic and structural indicators of emotionality was eminently appropriate.

Research Design and Procedures for Study I

Study I[1] was mainly an exploratory effort with the following related goals: first, to develop procedures and scoring categories relevant to the survey goals; then, to identify measurable variables that would be sensitive to the range of responses to the TAT cards; next, to construct criterion measures of psychological development and adjustment from information available in the Cycle II survey; and finally, to determine how the TAT variables relate to the criterion scales once constructed. As noted earlier, major attention was focused on these goals, and the sample selected from the total file of transcribed records was chosen, within each age-sex group, mainly with regard to completeness of data and quality of protocols available.

The general plan for this study involved the following steps: (1) development of experimental scoring manuals; (2) development of criterion measures of behaviors presumed to be measurable by analysis of the TAT protocols; (3) selection of experimental samples of children for the development and validation of the measurement scales; (4) scoring of the samples; and (5) validation of items, development of scales, and development of provisional norms based on the experimental samples.

Scoring Manuals.—Two related scoring manuals were developed; they are reproduced in appendix II. These consisted of the Structural Scoring Manual, designed to analyze oral language usage and style, and the Thematic Scoring Manual, which stressed evaluation derived from story content. While both were believed to have developmental as well as personality significance, the major emphasis was on language development in the Structural Manual and on aspects of emotionality and adjustment in the Thematic Manual.

A review of the literature[4] indicated that, although based on small samples, a number of previous efforts to analyze childrens' TAT productions quantitatively—in terms of length, parts of speech, and other formal characteristics—had produced developmental criteria of sufficient promise to encourage a large-scale effort along these lines. The Structural Scoring Manual developed for this type of quantitative analysis included 67 items for scoring in the following categories: time latency between instructions and response; total time; count of total words; frequency counts of about 20 parts of speech, defined in accordance with a standard text; a number of stylistic speech characteristics, such as questions, interpolations, dialogue, and contradictions; queer verbalizations; misperceptions of card content; compliance with instructions as to past, present, and future content; expressions of feeling and thinking; story outcomes; and the use of causally connected and purposefully connected statements. Previous studies have used many of these items; references to them are given in Sells' review.[4]

The 21 items to be scored in the Thematic Scoring Manual cover complexity of thematic elaboration; representation of manifest card content in stories; misperceptions and coherence of character reference; indicators of morbid mood, bizarre quality, religious content, confusion, escape, egocentrism, fantasy, fear, wealth, poverty, and projection; expression of hostility and affection in characteristic interpersonal relations; assignment of selected traits or behaviors to story characters (such as kind-loving, mean-rejecting, happy-glad, murder-killing); and analysis of goal orientations and story outcomes. The scoring of these items was categorical, in most cases, and areas of ambiguity were resolved by the adoption of arbitrary rules, which are given in the instructions for scoring in appendix II.

Development of TAT Scoring Procedures.— In this review only brief attention can be given to the problems that arose in the series of steps leading from raw protocols to a set of tentative norms. Nevertheless, some of these steps deserve mention because the quality of control exercised at each step in the analysis was in part responsible for the successful outcome of the study.

In order to remove irrelevant examiner variance from the protocols it was necessary to formulate strict rules to define both the beginning and the end of the scored protocol representing each story response. These are given in the Structural Scoring Manual, appendix II. According to these rules, a story is considered to begin at the point where the respondent starts to relate his response; this may be preceded by questions of the respondent or by efforts of the examiner to persuade the child to respond. Normally a story is considered to end when the subject stops or when he comments that the story is concluded. However, the rules provide general guidance to recognize leading questions or promptings by examiners which account for inadmissable content. Under these rules, post-story inquiries are excluded as well. Questions by the examiner to clarify mumbled speech, or comments of a supportive nature, such as "yes," "uh huh," which introduce no extraneous content, are not considered as bases for exclusion.

The problem of determining story boundaries is inseparable from that of defining the TAT response. Ideally, the examiner gives the instructions and then presents the TAT cards to the subject, one by one. The subject, in turn, tells a story, and then turns over the card, indicating that the story is completed. In fact, however, it was found that the story related is often a product of sometimes subtle and sometimes not so subtle interactions between the examiner and subject. These interactions include reinforcements given to the subject, promptings by the examiner, and questions by the subject concerning the story form and adequacy, before, during, and following the telling of the story.

Resolution of this problem is not an easy one. From the clinical viewpoint, the "extraneous," nonstandardized behaviors and the thematic production may be of equal value; story content given following a prompt may be considered a direct continuation of that given prior to the prompt. The problem is not unique with the TAT however; all measures employing unrestricted or open-ended responses are subject to wide variations in scores as a result of factors such as those mentioned above. The requirement for psychometric application is different, however, and the procedures accepted for the studies reported here have been to set up rather arbitrary standards for administration and responding and to accept only those responses or portions that fit within the predetermined standards.

Failure to produce a scorable story in response to any card stimulus was scored as a rejection for that card. Rejections were most easily scored when a child failed to respond at all. In some cases rejection was scored, despite a lengthy protocol, if application of the rules defining story boundaries rendered the response unscorable. In developing scores for sets of protocols, particularly in the case of word counts and counts of other specific categories of response, it was determined that the results would be more meaningful if rejections were left unscored than if scored as zero. When this was done, item scores were computed as averages across cards that could be scored.

One aspect of reliability concerned the consistency with which a single scorer assigned the story content to scoring categories from story to story, as well as his accuracy for scoring each story and variable. In addition, since there were several scorers, it was necessary that all scorers respond in a similar manner to a single given protocol. A second aspect concerned the degree to which items could be scored reliably by different scorers (scorer agreement). Reliability was easily obtained with word count items, but greater training and experience were required to gain suitable levels of reliability for some structural items, such as situation complexity (item 53 in Structural Scoring Manual, appendix II). An extensive report on the reliability of variables and on scorer agreement in this study is available elsewhere.[1,2] However, the essential findings of the reliability studies are briefly mentioned here. The median test-retest reliability coefficients of the five TAT cognitive scales that were developed (these scales are discussed under Results of Study I, below) were as follows:

Verbal productivity	.73
Maturity of language structure	.37
Conceptual maturity	.75
Maturity of language style	.60
Thematic scale	.43

The average interscorer agreement for eight scorers over all items in both scoring manuals was 94 percent.

The outcome of the efforts to achieve optimal "process control" in scoring was the selection of a set of variables for which acceptably reliable scoring could be obtained and the development of training procedures whereby such variables could be used reliably by nonprofessional personnel after 8 to 10 hours of supervised training.

Selection of Children.—Approximately 100 boys and 100 girls in each of the six age intervals 6 through 11 years were selected for the study. These children were selected from 17 locations or stands of the 40 stands[3] which constituted the entire Cycle II national survey. A description of both the HES Cycle II sample and the Study I sample is provided in appendix I.

Criterion Measures.—In order to have independent criterion measures of development and adjustment with which to validate the TAT scales that were developed, major effort was devoted to the availability of relevant information from other parts of the HES. In addition to the other psychological tests administered, it was possible to obtain copies of interviews with mothers and teachers as well as reports from school authorities containing information on health, social adjustment, grades, scholastic performance, and other aspects of general life adjustment of the children in the sample. Questionnaires used by the HES for gathering this information are discussed and reproduced in another NCHS publication.[3]

The criterion measures, or scales, employed in this study can be divided into two categories: development and adjustment. The developmental measures were chronologic age and an index of expected performance on cognitive functions, as measured by the Vocabulary and Block Design subtests of the WISC, Draw-A-Person, Reading and Arithmetic subtests of the WRAT, and by school reports of grade placement and scholastic performance.

4

Adjustment is at best a vague concept, but the home and school reports were exploited as completely as possible to develop scales reflecting aspects of personal and social adjustment defined in terms of the component items. Four criterion scales—reflecting social adjustment, health history (both as evaluated by the mother), and scholastic adjustment—were constructed from items in the various HES forms: scale 1, intellectual adjustment (from school form HES-243, Supplemental Information from School); scale 2, school social adjustment (from the same school form); scale 3, social maladjustment (from parent form HEW-257, Child's Medical History-Interviewer); and scale 4, medical history (from parent form HES-256, Child's Medical History-Parent). The questions used to define the criterion measures are discussed in the report on Study I.[1]

Because of the exploratory nature of the study, it was decided not to use factor analysis in the preliminary analysis of the criterion data. (The factor analytic approach was used in Study II.) Instead, items were chosen which reflected particular aspects of (1) adequacy of performance in school; (2) social adjustment to the school situation and to peers; (3) mother's evaluation of conduct, emotionality, and peer adjustment; and (4) developmental medical history. The four scales were then constructed as follows: items considered by the investigators to be similar in content were summed, then, individual items were correlated with these content-defined sum scores, and finally, items showing marked intercorrelations were selected to comprise the criterion scales. In addition to the foregoing, two derived scales were used—one, a linear combination of the last three scales, and the other, a weighted composite of the common factor contributions of the four scales.

Interpretation of the four original and two derived scales led to considerable speculation about the nature of the concept of adjustment. A noteworthy finding was the lack of substantial interrelation among the scales described above. The implication of these findings was either that the results reflected a series of independent, instrument-specific measures or that adjustment is a highly specific concept, tied closely to the background in which it is considered and to the scale of values along which it is measured. The converse term, maladjustment, would necessarily be generally meaningless unless the reference group and the norms of conformity for each source group were specified. The specificity of variance associated with each of these scales foreshadowed the results of the validation studies for the TAT thematic scale discussed below.

These criterion findings have implications for those who would study delinquency from the point of view that its roots lie in maladjustment as judged in domains such as the school and home. The lack of correlation among measures of these different aspects of adjustment raises questions concerning the wisdom of attempting to predict delinquency on the basis of poor adjustment in the home or school. It is no wonder that parents are often shocked upon finding that "Johnny, who has always been such a good boy," may also be a budding car thief.

Item Validation of Developmental Scales.— For the items scored on the Structural Manual, item scores were computed across the five cards, with the exception that card rejection was not included as a score. Item scores were then averaged for five or fewer cards. Each item was analyzed first for discrimination of chronologic age, using a one-way analysis of variance design. Correlations with age and with intelligence, reading, and arithmetic tests in the HES battery were computed for the total sample, for all items that discriminated age significantly.

Results of Study I

Extensive factor analytic investigations by age and sex groups led to the identification of five age-related scales, or factors. These factors were as follows:

I: Verbal productivity—This scale was defined in terms of numbers of verbs, nouns, pronouns, and other count items and measures of the quantity of spontaneous verbiage produced.

II: Maturity of language structure—This scale reflected differential use of parts of speech as a function of age and was defined chiefly in terms of adverbs, pronouns, and verbs.

As such it indicated age-related changes in proportional use of various structural elements of language.

III: Conceptual maturity—This scale was defined in terms of four variables: level of interpretation, situation complexity, outcome, and causally connected statements. It reflected the complexity of the conceptual content of the stories, independently of vocabulary complexity.

IV: Maturity of language style—This scale was defined by high loadings for proper nouns, first person pronouns, exclamations and comments, questions, dialogue, verbatim repetitions, and expletives. It was interpreted as a measure of stylistic variations in the forms of the story narrative.

V: Thematic—This scale was defined in terms of the following variables: escape, fantasy, fear, hostile antagonism, and the character attributes aggression, kind-loving, and happy-glad.

The maturity of language structure, maturity of language style, and conceptual maturity scales appeared related to a common factor apart from verbal productivity. The maturity of language style scale was less well defined than the four other (primary) scales.

Tentative analysis of the thematic items led to a scale which shared some common variance with the cognitive scales and which showed promise as an adjustment predictor.

Summary and Discussion of Study I

This study was undertaken for the purposes of developing (1) standardized scoring procedures and (2) useful measurement scales for a psychological test consisting of five TAT cards administered individually to a national probability sample of children in the United States in the age range 6 through 11 years. Criterion measures of development and adjustment were used to validate scoring items and measurement scales.

Two scoring manuals were developed, a Structural Manual and a Thematic Manual (appendix II). Acceptable levels of reliability were attained for the items in each manual. The items of the Structural Manual consisted of about 20 parts of speech, the number of words, a number of speech characteristics, and miscellaneous items, most of which were scored by quantitative counts. The items included in the Thematic Manual were based primarily on story content, such as complexity of theme, assignment of traits or behaviors to story characters, and expressions of hostility or affection in interpersonal relations.

Five TAT scales were constructed which were significantly associated with development or adjustment as measured by age and scales developed from questionnaire data. These scales are briefly described as follows: (I) verbal productivity, a factor-analytically derived, age-related scale based on measures reflecting quantity of verbal output; (II) maturity of language structure, an age-related measure of the relative frequency of use of certain language structures in the spoken language of the child; (III) conceptual maturity, an age-related measure of level of conceptual complexity of spoken language; (IV) maturity of language style, a moderately age-related scale based on common stylistic and expressive characteristics of spoken language; and (V) thematic scale, the best single TAT predictor of a criterion of adjustment, which was only moderately correlated with age.

While this exploratory study, in general, gave promise for the TAT mainly as an instrument to assess cognitive aspects of oral language development, there were some results which, while negative in tone, were informative as far as the process of behavioral prediction is concerned. These negative results were the approximately zero correlations among criterion clusters, and with a few exceptions, the relatively low intercorrelations between TAT scales and adjustment criterion measures. The criterion data tended to be composed of many unique clusters sharing little common variance. Consequently prediction of adjustment by the TAT scales was restricted. The lack of personality criterion data forestalled validating the TAT scales as personality measures.

PLAN OF STUDY II

Study II was in part a continuation of the objective of scale development reported in Study I, but this phase used more sophisticated analytic techniques. A second important objective was to provide national norms for the scales developed by using a probability subsample of the 7,119 children examined in Cycle II of the Health Examination Survey. In the developmental portion of the study, the total available sample of both studies was included in order to maximize the number of records on which the basic scales and statistical analyses were based and to increase reliability of the data. Only the probability subsample drawn from the entire Cycle II sample was used in computing the norms presented.

The analysis of TAT protocols and development of standardized scales progressed through several stages. The basic research design involved the following separate phases:

1. Development of criterion measures for validation of the TAT scales; the criteria were derived from information available from HES records as source documents.

2. Development of measurement scales for the TAT using structural and thematic variables for which scoring manuals had been developed and standardized in Study I.

3. Validation of measurement scales for the TAT by correlational analysis involving criterion measures, as well as age, sex, and race.

4. Development of norms based on the national probability sample.

The first three phases were conducted using a sample which combined cases from the Study I sample with those of the national probability sample. Inasmuch as the sample sizes varied in the several parts of this complex study, a detailed explanation of the Study II samples is presented in appendix I for the convenience of the reader. It is hoped that the presentation will avoid confusion and unnecessary cross-checking to account for variations.

Criterion Data

The Division of Health Examination Statistics of the National Center for Health Statistics furnished the following data on each child in both Study I and II: age at the time of testing; sex; race-ethnic status; family background; scores on WISC Vocabulary and Block Design tests; scores on the Draw-A-Person Test derived from the Goodenough-Harris scales; scores on the Wide Range Achievement Test, 1965 Revision, Reading and Arithmetic subtests; and forms containing information gathered from parents and school personnel relating to the child's health history, current behavior, adjustment, and school performance. (An earlier NCHS publication[3] describes the methods and shows the forms used for collecting these data. The specific questions and answers used in this study are shown in appendix III.) These data were available on 2,012 children in the combined sample and were used in the development of the criterion measures described next.

Four criterion scales, identical in item composition to those described in Study I (reference 1, pp. 25-29, and reference 5), were computed for 2,012 cases of the total sample. (Six cases with missing criterion data were excluded from the criterion analysis.)

In order to expand and possibly to improve on the criterion analysis reported in Study I, it was decided to factor analyze matrices of criterion variables for the total sample. Initially, a matrix of 68 items was generated including:

1. The four criterion scales developed in Study I (see pp. 4 and 5.)

2. Forty-nine behavior adjustment, medical history, and school performance items, used to develop the above four scales in Study I.

3. Five intellect-related scales: WISC Block Design, WISC Vocabulary, Draw-A-Person, WRAT Reading, and WRAT Arithmetic (also used in Study I).

4. The following five additional measures, not used in Study I: skipped a grade, repeated a grade, rural versus not rural, family income, and foreign language in the home.

5. Five control variables: age in months, sex, race, sample I versus sample II in the replication design, and manually recorded versus transcribed stories.

The four original criterion scales were included in the correlation matrix for the purpose of comparison with the earlier results as well as for assessment of the scales for internal consistency and validity. However, the four scales were excluded from the factor analysis because their spurious (part-whole) relationship with the items would have confounded the factor analytic results; afterwards, they were correlated with the factor analytically derived criterion scales.

The WISC and WRAT subtests and the DAP as well as the five additional conceptually related items (skipped a grade, repeated a grade, rural vs. not rural, family income, and foreign language in the home) were expected to cluster with the items comprising criterion scale 1 of Study I, intellectual adjustment.

Three of the five control variables (age, sex, and race) were included in the factor analysis in order to assess their association with the derived factors.

TAT Analysis and Scoring

The analysis of the TAT data represented the largest and most demanding task in this study. Technical adequacy of the recordings of the transcribed protocols was an important consideration in the selection of cases in Study I. In that study the emphasis was on scale development, and an effort was made to maximize the usefulness of records while less emphasis was placed on sampling adequacy. As a result, every child included in the first study had actually produced a scorable protocol and had complete criterion data. In the present study some information was unfortunately lost due to technical problems. A review of sample children for whom inadequate data necessitated omission is presented in appendix I.

The Structural and Thematic Manuals (appendix II) described in the earlier study[1] were used to score all 2,018 cases, including the additional cases ($n = 1,022$) selected for the present study for whom TAT protocols were available. Two teams of scorers scored the entire set of additional protocols; each team included a senior and a junior scorer. The junior scorers were undergraduate college women with backgrounds in English grammar, and their duties were to score all "count" type items. The senior scorers were women with college degrees who had received training as scorers during Study I; their duties were to score the remaining items and to supervise the work of the junior scorers.

Following is a brief resume of the extent of card rejection, which substantiates points made in the earlier study regarding the requirement for objective standards in delineating story boundaries. Furthermore, as shown later, card rejection was a key defining variable in one of the cognitive factors (factor III, conceptual maturity) developed for this version of the TAT.

Card Rejections.—Story boundaries were defined as in Study I (see pp. 3 and 4) and as outlined in the Structural Scoring Manual in appendix II. Failure to produce a scorable story in response to any card stimulus was recorded as a rejection for that card. Rejections were also scored as in Study I (see page 4), with one exception: in the present study a variable denoting the number of card rejections was included in the analysis. Cases with rejections on all five cards were dropped from Study I as a result of a clerical error; four such cases were included in Study II. A tabulation of rejections, by TAT card, for age-race-sex groups in the total sample ($n = 2,018$) is shown in table 1.[a]

Tests for the significance of differences between independent proportions[6] were computed to evaluate the relationship of sex and race[b] to rejections for each of the TAT cards. These results, shown in table 2, indicate that: (1) there were no significant differences between boys and

---

[a]Tables 1-10 are supplementary tables that appear in a separate section, beginning on page 25.

[b]The numbers of children in the two racial groups—white and black—sampled in this study are given in appendix I. The white group included two oriental children.

girls within the white group; (2) a significantly higher proportion of the 99 black girls than the 96 black boys rejected cards 5 and 8 BM; (3) no significant differences occurred between boys and girls for the total sample; (4) no significant differences occurred between the white and black samples of boys; and (5) a larger proportion of black girls than white girls rejected card 16 (the blank card), as did the total sample of blacks in comparison with the total sample of whites. Black children rejected only card 16 more frequently than did white children.

The relationship between age and card rejection was investigated for the samples of white boys and girls and for the total sample of boys and girls. The numbers of cases within age categories for the black sample were too small to obtain stable relationships. Kendall's coefficient of concordance,[7] however, indicated that the proportions of card rejections were significantly related to age level for white boys ($W = .59$, $p < .01$), that is, there was a decreasing number of rejections with increasing age, but were not significant for all boys, white girls, or all girls.

The five TAT cards differed in relation to the frequency of card rejections. For the total sample of boys and girls ($n = 2,018$), the numbers and proportions of rejections, by card, were: card 16, 137 rejections, 6.8 percent; card 1, 73 rejections, 3.6 percent; card 2, 57 rejections, 2.8 percent; card 8 BM, 47 rejections, 2.3 percent; card 5, 26 rejections, 1.3 percent. This pattern was extremely stable across the four sex-race subgroups, as indicated by Kendall's coefficient of concordance ($W = .98$, $p < .01$).

DEVELOPMENT OF CRITERION SCALES

In the development of criterion scales, product-moment correlations were computed among the 68 criterion variables discussed on pp. 7 and 8 and enumerated in table 3. This intercorrelation matrix (excluding the variables representing the four criterion scales from Study I) was factor analyzed using the principal components solution[8] followed by a varimax rotation[9] to orthogonal simple structure. Results of this analysis are shown in table 4 which presents the rotated factor matrix based on a five-factor solution. The five factors are defined as follows, using salient loadings as a basis for factor definition.

Criterion Factor I—School Adjustment

Five items were selected to define this factor: grade repeated, special or remedial class attended, attentiveness to class work, intellectual ability, and academic performance (table A). (The information was obtained directly from the children's schools by use of questions from HES form 243, shown in appendix III.) The content of these marker variables suggested that some measure of "school adjustment" was being obtained. The factor loadings of the items ranged from .86 (academic performance) to .43 (grade repeated). With the exception of the item "grade repeated" this scale is identical in composition to the intellectual adjustment scale of Study I. To obtain a score on this scale (factor) the unweighted scores on each of the defining variables were summed. A similar composite score was obtained on each of the criterion scales discussed below.

Criterion Factor II—Poor Health

Factor analysis of 26 health items derived from the HES Medical History form, No. 256, shown in appendix III (variables 18-43 in table 3), revealed that only eight items from the Medical History form were of salient importance as health criteria. Based on these marker items, this factor is designated here as "poor health"; the eight items composing it are summarized in table A.

The information for the items on this factor was obtained primarily from interview reports contributed by the mothers of the children and may thus reflect some bias. As a group, the items do give a picture of illnesses which contribute to poor health of the children. Loadings indicate that the two "present health" items contributed the greatest amount of variance to the poor health factor, followed by history of measles, serious accident or injury, other allergies, hay fever, kidney trouble, and speech defects.

Table A. Variables used to define the five criterion factors: scoring, means, standard deviations (SD), and factor loadings

Criterion factor and variable	HES form and question number[2]	Scoring	Mean	SD	Factor loading
Factor I—School adjustment					
6. Academic performance	243-#19	0—above average 1—average 2—below average	0.96	0.69	.86
5. Intellectual ability	243-#18	0—above average 1—average 2—below average	0.91	0.65	.85
3. Class attended	243-#8	0—gifted 1—normal classes 2—slow learners 3—handicapped	0.10	0.49	.71
4. Attentiveness	243-#12	0—above average 1—average 2—below average	1.00	0.66	.66
1. Grade repeated	243-#4	0—no 1—yes	0.10	0.30	.43
Factor II—Poor health					
39. Present health problems	256-#21	0—no 1—yes	0.19	0.39	.58
18. Present health status	256-#20	0—very good, good 1—fair, poor	0.06	0.23	.54
33. Measles (severity)	256-#33	0—not severe 1—severe	0.06	0.24	.48
22. Serious accident or injury	256-#28	0—no 1—yes	0.17	0.38	.44
35. Other allergies	256-#35	0—no 1—yes	0.11	0.31	.31
34. Hay fever	256-#35	0—no 1—yes	0.06	0.25	.29
36. Kidney trouble	256-#35	0—no 1—yes	0.04	0.19	.28
40. Speech defect	256-#50	0—no	0.05	0.21	.28
Factor III—Intellectual development					
61. Age in months	...	...	107.73	20.52	.82
67. WISC Vocabulary raw score	...	actual score	25.49	9.78	.82
60. WRAT Arithmetic score	...	actual score	27.28	8.35	.80
59. WRAT Reading score	...	actual score	51.47	19.61	.79
66. Goodenough-Harris score	...	actual score	23.28	7.68	.73
68. WISC Block Design raw score	...	actual score	12.77	10.43	.71
Factor IV—Social adjustment					
53. Interchild relations	257-#15	0—well liked 1—average 2—has difficulty	0.56	0.57	.60
52. New friends	257-#14	0—very outgoing 1—above average 2—shy	0.72	0.75	.53
56. Tension level	257-#18	0—calm, relaxed 1—tense, nervous	0.16	0.36	.52
57. Temper	257-#19	0—rare, occasionally 1—strong, easily lost	0.17	0.37	.47
55. Trauma	257-#17	0—no 1—yes	0.25	0.43	.32
51. Range of food tastes	257-#5	0—eats most 1—somewhat and very fussy	0.23	0.42	.31
Factor V—Emotional disturbance					
11. Aggression	243-#14	0—normal 1-6—number of aggressive behaviors checked	0.27	0.77	.71
9. Overall adjustment	243-#11	0—very well adjusted 1—no adjustment problem 2—adjustment problem	0.99	0.58	.54
8. Emotionally disturbed	243-#8	0—no 1—yes	0.04	0.21	.49
10. Motor activity	243-#13	0—normal 1—restless or too quiet	0.31	0.46	.36

[1] The original numbers assigned to the variables have been retained, even though they appear out of numerical order for this grouping by factors.

[2] The questions from the appropriate HES forms are shown in appendix III.

Criterion Factor III—Intellectual Development

The third factor was designated "intellectual development" (table A) in view of the high loadings of the five intellectual measures. Age in months tied with the WISC Vocabulary raw score for the highest loading on this factor, emphasizing the developmental significance of these intellectual scales. The WISC Block Design score contributed least to this intellectual development factor, while the WISC Vocabulary and the WRAT Reading and Arithmetic scores appeared to be of slightly greater importance in total contribution to factor variance. Age correlated .50 with the Block Design score in contrast to .79, .69, and .62 with the Arithmetic, Reading, and Vocabulary scores, respectively.

Criterion Factor IV—Social Adjustment

The six items (table A) representing factor IV were based on judgmental ratings (similar in this respect to those in the poor health scale), reported by the child's mother to the survey interviewer (HES form 257, appendix III). This factor was designated "social adjustment" to reflect the importance of the six defining items to the child's social development. Interchild (peer) relations and the ability to meet new friends contributed most to the Social Adjustment factor. Four other items included were tension level, experience of trauma, temper, and range of food tastes.

Criterion Factor V—Emotional Disturbance

Aggression, overall adjustment problems, emotional disturbance, and amount of motor activity defined this factor as shown in table A. These defining variables were derived from questions in school form HES 243, shown in appendix III. Aggression was the dominant item in this factor and had the largest correlation with the criterion scale 2, school social adjustment, of Study I. The loadings of the items ranged from .71 to .36; motor activity contributed the least among the defining variables.

Relationships Among Criterion Factor Scores and Age, Sex, and Race

The correlations among the composite scores on the criterion factors are shown in table B. The school adjustment and emotional disturbance factors were most highly related with a

Table B. Correlations among the composite scores on the criterion factors and age, sex, and race

Variable	Variable							
	1	2	3	4	5	6	7	8
1. Criterion factor I—school adjustment--------	1.00							
2. Criterion factor II—poor health---------------	-0.05	1.00						
3. Criterion factor III—intellectual development---	0.28	0.02	1.00					
4. Criterion factor IV—social adjustment--------	0.12	-0.20	0.03	1.00				
5. Criterion factor V—emotional disturbance-------	-0.44	0.08	-0.09	-0.13	1.00			
6. Age-----------------------	-0.03	-0.05	0.77	-0.02	0.03	1.00		
7. Sex-----------------------	0.16	-0.03	0.03	0.09	-0.19	0.02	1.00	
8. Race-----------------------	0.07	0.03	0.15	0.07	0.06	0.02	-0.01	1.00

correlation of -.44. The negative sign here indicates that a high rating on school adjustment was associated with a low or poor rating on emotional adjustment. Criterion factor III (intellectual development) was the only factor with a substantial correlation with age (.77). Since age was one of the defining variables for criterion factor III, this relationship was spuriously inflated. Nevertheless, when age was partialed out of the factor, the correlation with age was reduced only to .64. The remaining four criterion measures were virtually uncorrelated with age. Sex (female) was positively correlated with the school adjustment criterion factor ($r = .16$) and negatively correlated ($r = -.19$) with emotional disturbance. (In this case, the negative sign indicates that girls were not associated with being emotionally disturbed.) These correlations are assumed to give evidence for the position that culturally defined behavior roles for young girls coincide more readily with behavioral norms, also culturally decreed, for proper school conduct than do those behavioral roles defined for young boys.

Another cultural byproduct may be the basis for the positive correlation ($r = .15$) between criterion factor III, intellectual development, and race (white). The relatively small percent of variance (2.25) in intellectual development is likely a cultural-developmental phenomenon, related in part to differential exposure to the predominant language community.

Relationships of Age With Items Used To Define Criterion Factors

Mean scores and standard deviations for the 68 criterion items, by factor, in 2-year age and sex groups are shown in table 5. Many of the criterion items showed consistent linear relationships across the three age groups, for each sex. However, there were a number of items which showed a curvilinear relationship with age. For example, item number 11 (aggression) represents a curvilinear function across age groups: the aggression mean for boys, ages 6 and 7, is 0.34, followed by an increase to 0.49 for the middle ages (8 and 9) and then a decrease to 0.38 for the older ages (10 and 11). The same relationship for this item is apparent among girls,

except that the marked decline was not obtained among older girls.

DEVELOPMENT OF THE TAT SCALES—STRUCTURAL AND THEMATIC DATA

Analysis of the structural and thematic data derived from the story protocols occurred in two phases. The first phase consisted of a correlational analysis of scores on most of the items from both the Structural and Thematic Manuals (appendix II). A factor analysis was performed to identify the dimensions relevant to the TAT responses. For phase one, 87 word count and thematic items were selected. Nineteen items included in the scoring manuals were eliminated, principally on the basis of infrequent occurrence.

Phase two involved selection of those items defining the principal dimensions isolated in phase one (31 items in all) and refactoring of the correlation matrix of this reduced set of items. In terms of psychological meaning it was assumed that the list of 87 items actually represented only a few dimensions. The two-phase analysis was conducted on the basis of such an assumption and appears to have been justified by the results. Computation of these factors had the advantages of reducing the variables to a more manageable number and of simplifying the final steps in determination of the language and thematic scales.

Several groups of variables were eliminated or combined in reducing the number of items from 87 to 31. First, it was decided to eliminate those variables having negligible or zero loadings on the five factors accepted after the initial analysis of the 87 items as well as those having low to zero intercorrelations with other variables. Second, it appeared appropriate to combine certain related items which had very low means. For example, four items measuring various aspects of hostile antagonism were combined into a single item, preserving the common aspects of their TAT responses and at the same time providing a more reliable measure of manifest hostility. Third, some items found in clusters with extremely high intercorrelations resulting from statistical interdependencies were excluded. An example is the elimination of *number of words*, since this item was inevitably highly correlated with the other word count items. A second example involves the four items dealing with goal behavior. Since they had very high intercorrelations, three of the four were considered redundant and were therefore removed.

Means and standard deviations for the 31 selected variables plus some additional variables of interest are reported in table 6. The large variances reflect the effect of aging over a 6-year age range which includes several developmental levels. Additionally, several variables listed in table 6 had zero as modal scores, giving rise to markedly skewed distributions.

The intercorrelations among the scores on the 31 items selected in phase two are shown in table 7. (The items in this table are ordered to reflect clusters of variables defining each of the major factors resulting from the analysis discussed below.) These intercorrelations were computed on a sample of 1,910 subjects (excluding 102 subjects from combined sample I and II). The 31 by 31 correlation matrix was factor analyzed, using the principal component method, with unities in the principal diagonal. Factor extraction was halted when eigenvalues fell below 1.0 and seven factors were extracted. However, only the first six factors were readily interpretable, and these were rotated using the varimax method. The rotated factor matrix is presented in table 8.

The six TAT factors retained accounted for 63.63 percent of the total variance. Factor I accounted for 34.86 percent of the variance. This was followed by a sharp decline to 7.96 percent in factor II. The six rotated factors were accepted as the best representation of the variance in the matrix of intercorrelations. The variance accounted for by each of the rotated factors is indicated in table 8.

The salient marker variables were used to interpret and define the factors. Table C shows the items for each of the six TAT factors and their respective loadings. In this · table, all loadings of .30 or greater are listed. For the purposes of computing composite scores, however, only those with the highest loadings were used. This issue is discussed at length in a later section.

TAT Factor I—Verbal Productivity

Table C shows the variables whose factor loadings on factor I were at least .30. The unweighted standard scores on the first six variables listed were used to compute composite scores for this factor. The label "verbal productivity" was chosen for at least two reasons. First, three of the six composite-forming variables—corrections, pauses, and repetitions—reflect what might be termed monitoring and mechanical functions associated with the production of the verbal protocol. Since these three variables were measured in terms of frequency of occurrence of the respective functions, it is not surprising that they show uniform and highly similar correlations with other productivity variables. This would also account for the loadings on this factor of pronouns, single verbs, common nouns, and possessive adjectives. Another reason for the designation of this factor as "verbal productivity" was that the items concern story construction and formation. They reflect attempts by the children to develop stories that emphasize proper organization of characters, places, and situations. The presence of both past and future reference is taken as an indication of efforts to give temporal boundaries to the stories; these variables reflect story content prior to and subsequent to the content manifested in the TAT cards. Among the grammatical classes of words, use of adverbs, in particular, gives the story action a fine-grained quality indicative of a high level of competence in manipulating the language. Finally factor I is believed to represent a facility to use and produce language in a way that is culturally defined as competent and effective.

In summarizing these data, it should be emphasized that factor I was of overwhelming importance relative to the other factors identified. The principal component solution indicated that a little over 50 percent of the total variance accounted for was attributable to factor I. The varimax rotation lent greater interpretability to the factors but, in the process, redistributed the variance among the factors. A great deal of the variance provided by factor I shifted to the other factors so that in the rotated solution its relative importance was reduced.

Table C. Variables used to define the six TAT factors and their factor loadings

TAT factor and variable[1]	Item number in scoring manual[2]	Factor loading
Factor I—Verbal productivity		
4. Corrections[3]	48 (SM)	.80
6. Future reference[3]	60 (SM)	.73
5. Past reference[3]	58 (SM)	.72
2. Pauses[3]	46 (SM)	.69
1. Adverbs[3]	20 (SM)	.58
3. Verbatim repetitions[3]	47 (SM)	.51
29. Pronouns	28 (SM)	.46
30. Single verbs	32 (SM)	.46
28. Common nouns	24 (SM)	.41
12. Situation complexity	53 (SM)	.40
27. Possessive adjectives	19 (SM)	.38
17. Outcome	63 (SM)	.37
24. Egocentrism	11 (TM)	.31
Factor II—Dysphoric mood		
8. Death[3]	20h (TM)	.86
9. Murder-killing[3]	20i (TM)	.82
7. Unhappy outcome[3]	64(2) (SM)	.61
23. Bizarre theme	7 (TM)	.33
Factor III—Conceptual maturity		
13. Present reference[3]	59 (SM)	.94
10. Rejection[3]	1 (SM)	.93
11. Level of interpretation[3]	65 (SM)	.65
12. Situation complexity[3]	53 (SM)	.60
Factor IV—Narrative fluency		
17. Outcome[3]	63 (SM)	.78
14. Happy outcome[3]	64(1) (SM)	.74
15. Causally connected statements[3]	66 (SM)	.64
16. Expression of feeling[3]	61 (SM)	.58
19. Happy-glad (character attribute)[3]	20d (TM)	.44
20. Goal behavior[3]	21 (TM)	.44
18. Kind-loving (character attribute)[3]	20a (TM)	.38

[1] The original numbers assigned to the variables have been retained, even though they appear out of numerical order for this grouping by factors. See appendix II for information on how the numbered items were scored.
[2] SM = Structural Manual, TM = Thematic Manual; both manuals appear in appendix II.
[3] Variable used to compute composite scores.

Table C. Variables used to define the six TAT factors and their factor loadings—Con.

TAT factor and variable[1]	Item number in scoring manual[2]	Factor loading
Factor IV—Narrative fluency—Con.		
11. Level of interpretation	65(SM)	.57
12. Situation complexity	53(SM)	.52
6. Future reference	60(SM)	.43
29. Pronouns	28(SM)	.38
27. Possessive adjectives	19(SM)	.37
7. Unhappy outcome	64(2)(SM)	.36
30. Single verbs	32(SM)	.34
28. Common nouns	24(SM)	.32
5. Past reference	58(SM)	.30
Factor V—Emotionality		
25. Mean-rejecting (character attribute)[3]	20b(TM)	.67
21. Antagonism[3]	18(TM)	.64
26. Aggression[3]	20e(TM)	.59
23. Bizarre theme[3]	7(TM)	.57
24. Egocentrism[3]	11(TM)	.44
22. Morbid mood quality[3]	6(TM)	.39
20. Goal behavior	21(TM)	.49
18. Kind-loving (character attribute)	20a(TM)	.35
Factor VI—Verbal fluency		
28. Common nouns[3]	24(SM)	.72
30. Single verbs[3]	32(SM)	.72
29. Pronouns[3]	28(SM)	.68
27. Possessive adjectives[3]	19(SM)	.65
31. Dialogue[3]	49,50(SM)	.65
3. Verbatim repetitions	47(SM)	.43
15. Causally connected statements	66(SM)	.40
1. Adverbs	20(SM)	.39
18. Kind-loving (character attribute)	20a(TM)	.36
19. Happy-glad (character attribute)	20d(TM)	.32

[1]The original numbers assigned to the variables have been retained, even though they appear out of numerical order for this grouping by factors. See appendix II for information on how the numbered items were scored.
[2]SM = Structural Manual, TM = Thematic Manual; both manuals appear in appendix II.
[3]Variable used to compute composite scores.

TAT Factor II—Dysphoric Mood

Examination of the three variables defining factor II (shown in table C) and their loadings would suggest this factor to be a result of spurious dependency between death and murder-killing. However, this factor also emerged in a trial analysis when murder-killing was excluded from the variable list. Nevertheless, the paucity of variables defining factor II, plus the presence of a conceptually related factor (see factor V), led to the judgment that factor II was of relatively minor importance. It seems a reasonable hypothesis that the factor was strongly a product of responses to TAT card 8 BM.

TAT Factor III—Conceptual Maturity

This factor was rather sharply defined by four variables, shown in table C. The designation of this factor as "conceptual maturity" reflects two important aspects of this factor. One is that the factor measures the extent to which the children understood the instructions and requirements of the storymaking situation; the second is that it measures the qualitative graduations in the structure of the stories themselves. Level of interpretation, which indicates the extent to which the behavior of the characters is given a meaningful basis, and situation complexity, which indicates finesse in depicting story plot through temporal and situational variation, were the two variables used to specify the quality of story structure.

TAT Factor IV—Narrative Fluency

In table C it can be seen by the nature of the large number of variables loading on factor IV that it is a complex dimension. The name for this dimension was chosen to reflect the interpretation that this factor represents those stories, particularly those positive in outlook, in which thematic elements make sharply defined appearances within the boundaries of well-conceived and well-developed stories. It may be noted that the two "depth measures" (level of interpretation and situation complexity) loaded highly on factor IV; these variables were not included in the composite list, however, because of their inclusion in the composite for factor III. Nevertheless, by the magnitude of their loadings on

this factor, they also contributed to the interpretation suggested for factor IV.

TAT Factor V—Emotionality

Two possible interpretations are suggested for factor V, as summarized in table C. One is that the factor to some degree stands as a negatively toned counterpart to factor IV. Thus, factor V would represent negatively conceived stories. However, noticeably absent from factor V were any of the variables representing structural or conceptual organization. Thus an alternative, related interpretation is that this factor concerns chiefly the expression of aggressive, hostile ideas and, more generally, emotionality on the part of the subject. It will be noted that goal behavior was not included among the composite variables. Earlier analyses in which fewer factors were rotated suggested that it was more appropriate to include goal behavior as a composite variable for factor IV.

TAT Factor VI—Verbal Fluency

As shown in table C the chief defining variables for this factor were the count items for grammatical forms. In evaluating the results, it should be kept in mind that a large proportion of the variance reflected in the TAT measures is accounted for in terms of the amount of verbiage produced in the stories. The more words that were produced, the greater the chance that expression of plot and character development would take place. While it is certainly possible to produce complex stories with relative brevity, the empirical findings of this study show consistent, high positive correlations between the production measures (count items) and items measuring other aspects of the responses. The first principal component resembled what would be the effect of combining into one factor the loadings of the marker variables on the rotated factors I, III, and VI. In its unrotated form the first principal component clearly represented verbal production. In addition the variables defining factor VI retained substantial loadings on the rotated factor I. Although the two factors are thus related, factor VI is interpreted as representing the verbal fluency component of the count items, whereas factor I is considered to reflect the component of verbal productivity.

VALIDATION OF THE TAT SCALES

The research reported in the preceding sections resulted in the construction of five criterion measures of development and adjustment and six TAT scales, or factors, derived from analysis of the story protocols. The five criterion measures representing intellectual development and adjustment were based on factor analysis of 64 variables derived from tests and background information collected in Cycle II of the HES. Four of the criterion scales reflected essentially uncorrelated facets of adjustment and were defined by the behavior adjustment, medical history, and school performance information made available from the Cycle II documents. The remaining criterion scale, the intellectual development criterion factor (factor III in table A), represented a composite of the WISC, WRAT,

and Goodenough-Harris scales and age. The six TAT scales, representing aspects of language development and emotionality expressed in the story protocols, were constructed on the basis of a factor analysis of 31 structural and thematic scoring variables. The validity of the TAT scales as measures of psychological value was analyzed on the basis of their relationships to the criterion factors and to age, sex, and race.

Relationships were analyzed among the composite scores on the six TAT factors and among the scores on the five criterion measures, as well as between TAT and criterion factors. As stated previously, individual scores for the six TAT factors were formed by summing the unweighted standard scores of the defining items for each factor. Ages were recorded in months. Intercorrelations among the 14 variables were then computed for the total sample of 1,910 children. The results are shown in table D.

Table D. Correlations among TAT predictor composite scores, criterion composite scores, age, sex, and race

Variable	Variable													
	1	2	3	4	5	6	7	8	9	10	11	12	13	14
1. TAT factor I— verbal productivity	1.00													
2. TAT factor II— dysphoric mood	0.19	1.00												
3. TAT factor III— conceptual maturity	0.42	0.20	1.00											
4. TAT factor IV— narrative fluency	0.43	0.15	0.37	1.00										
5. TAT factor V— emotionality	0.26	0.29	0.15	0.26	1.00									
6. TAT factor VI— verbal fluency	0.54	0.23	0.31	0.48	0.26	1.00								
7. Criterion factor I—school adjustment	0.12	0.00	0.09	0.15	0.00	0.15	1.00							
8. Criterion factor II—poor health	-0.01	-0.01	0.00	0.00	0.00	-0.01	-0.05	1.00						
9. Criterion factor III—intellectual development	0.35	0.03	0.24	0.35	0.06	0.35	0.28	0.02	1.00					
10. Criterion factor IV—social adjustment	0.03	0.00	0.02	0.04	0.00	0.05	0.12	-0.20	0.03	1.00				
11. Criterion factor V—emotional disturbance	-0.02	0.02	-0.03	-0.06	0.01	-0.05	-0.44	0.08	-0.09	-0.13	1.00			
12. Age	0.23	0.02	0.18	0.29	0.06	0.27	-0.03	-0.05	0.77	-0.02	0.03	1.00		
13. Sex	0.01	-0.03	0.02	0.06	-0.06	0.07	0.16	-0.03	0.03	0.09	-0.19	0.02	1.00	
14. Race	0.22	0.01	0.02	-0.02	-0.01	0.07	0.07	0.03	0.15	0.07	0.06	0.02	-0.01	1.00

Relationships Among Composite Scores on TAT Factors, Age, Sex, and Race

It may be recalled that in forming the TAT predictor factors care was taken not to include any variable in more than one composite. This was done to eliminate spuriously high correlations between factors due to artifactual dependencies. Even so, it is readily apparent through observation of the intercorrelations among the composite scores on the TAT factors shown in table D that substantial correlations remain. The factors may be thought of as representing two clusters, one pertaining to cognitive-verbal factors, and the other, to an emotional-hostile expression factor. The average correlation among the TAT cognitive-verbal factors I, III, IV, and VI is .43; the correlations range from .31 between factors III and VI to .54 between factors I and VI. Scores on the dysphoric mood and emotionality factors correlated .29.

Turning to the correlations with age, sex, and race, it can be observed that the four TAT "cognitive" factors show substantial correlations with age. Narrative fluency shows the highest correlation with age ($r = .29$) among the four. Sex is not appreciably correlated with any of the TAT factors. On the other hand, there is a substantial correlation between race and verbal productivity ($r = .22$). White children tended to obtain higher scores on this factor than did black children.

Relationships Between TAT and Criterion Composites

Validity of the TAT factors was assessed in terms of their relationships, as measured by product-moment correlation, with the five criterion factors and with age, sex, and race. As shown in table D, scores on all six of the TAT factors correlate near zero with the criterion factors labeled poor health, social adjustment, and emotional disturbance. The four cognitive TAT factors (I, III, IV, and VI) are relatively highly correlated with the intellectual development criterion factor (III) and are moderately correlated with the school adjustment factor (I). The correlations of the four cognitive TAT factors with these two criterion factors are all

significant beyond the .01 level. The emotionality factor has essentially zero correlations with the school adjustment composite score and the intellectual development composite score.

The low validity coefficients for the TAT emotionality factor were disappointing. The evidence indicates that it is not a measure of maladjustment, as reflected by the criteria available. The appearance of this factor in the factor matrix is clear, and the consistency of the items loaded supports the interpretation that it is a substantive factor, even though the validation with external criteria has not been established. Apparently the factor represents an expression of hostility and destructiveness in fantasy which is not openly reflected in real-life situations. Pending further study of behavioral validity in relation to independent criteria, it must be considered provisionally as fantasy construction.

Correlated and Uncorrelated TAT Factors

For purposes of the following discussion a distinction will be made between the terms TAT *composite scores* and TAT *factor scores*. In the preceding discussions all references to scores on TAT factors have been to composite scores based on unweighted sums of marker variables. There is an advantage, however, in the use of factor scores, which are orthogonal; that is, they are mutually uncorrelated. (There may be substantial intercorrelations among simple composite scores.) The disadvantage of factor scores is that they are laborious to compute while composite scores can be directly computed using the tables provided in appendix IV. For the purposes of interpretive clarity, the preceding analyses were supplemented by an analysis based on the use of orthogonal TAT factors.

Computation of TAT Factor Scores. —The subject's z scores for the 31 TAT variables were converted into six factor scores by use of two matrix equations:

$$W = R^{-1} F \qquad (1)$$

$$P = Z' W \qquad (2)$$

In equation (1) the weight matrix *(W)* was formed by multiplying the inverse of the correlation matrix (R^{-1}) by the matrix of vari-

Table E. Correlations of orthogonal TAT factor scores with TAT and criterion composite scores and with age, sex, and race

Variable	TAT orthogonal factors					
	I	II	III	IV	V	VI
1. TAT factor I—verbal productivity——————	.88	.07	.11	.24	.12	.32
2. TAT factor II—dysphoric mood—————————	.12	.94	.06	.10	.16	.07
3. TAT factor III—conceptual maturity————	.28	.11	.63	.56	.11	.25
4. TAT factor IV—narrative fluency———————	.21	-.02	.20	.81	.25	.37
5. TAT factor V—emotionality—————————————	.19	.20	.05	.09	.92	.14
6. TAT factor VI—verbal fluency———————————	.41	.12	.13	.35	.20	.77
7. Criterion factor I—school adjustment——	.12	-.03	.01	.22	.05	.06
8. Criterion factor II—poor health———————	-.01	-.01	-.03	.02	.00	-.02
9. Criterion factor III—intellectual development—————————————————————————	.33	-.06	.15	.45	.02	.10
10. Criterion factor IV—social adjustment—	.02	.00	.00	.05	.01	.04
11. Criterion factor V—emotional disturbance————————————————————————	-.01	.04	.00	-.10	.03	-.03
12. Age—————————————————————————————————————	.19	-.05	.14	.38	.05	.09
13. Sex—————————————————————————————————————	-.02	-.02	-.06	.14	.14	.09
14. Race————————————————————————————————————	.37	-.01	-.03	-.06	.06	-.07

max factor loadings (F). The weight matrix is presented in appendix V as table IX. In equation (2) the factor scores (P) were obtained by multiplying the z scores (Z') by the weight matrix. As the final step, correlations between these orthogonal factor scores and other variables were obtained.

Correlations of Orthogonal Factor Scores With Criterion Composite Scores, Age, Sex, and Race.—In the lower half of table E, the correlations between the TAT orthogonal factor scores and criterion composite scores, age, sex, and race, are shown. The intercorrelations among TAT factor scores are not reported, as they are equal to zero; the intercorrelations among criterion measures, age, sex, and race have already been given in tables B and D. Tables D and E should be compared carefully.

In table D verbal productivity, narrative fluency, and verbal fluency correlated equally with criterion factor III, intellectual development ($r = .35$). However, because these TAT com-

posite scores were themselves intercorrelated, it was desirable to obtain a clearer picture of their relationship with intellectual development. In table E it can be seen that the correlation of verbal productivity with intellectual development (.33) remains essentially unchanged, while that of verbal fluency with intellectual development (.10) is considerably reduced. On the other hand, there was a substantial increase (from .35 to .45) in the correlation between intellectual development and factor IV, narrative fluency. An explanation of the differences may be that all of the unweighted composites contained variance associated with productivity. With the factor scores, on the other hand, the productivity variance was restricted to factor I, while the two fluency measures were restricted to factors IV and VI. Previous empirical evidence supports the view that verbal fluency does not tend to correlate with intellectual level measures.

There is a marked increase in the correlation between race (white) and verbal productivity, in going from the TAT composite score in table D (.22) to the TAT factor score in table E (.37). The positive correlation between verbal productivity and race, white children rating higher on this factor, gives substance to the interpretation advanced earlier concerning race and intellectual development. The verbal productivity factor is seen in part as an indicator of the linguistic milieu with which children are most familiar. Black children, whose linguistic surroundings often differ from those of white children, have less contact with the prevailing patterns of English expression than do whites. Consequently, while the linguistic skills of blacks in their dialect may be comparable with those of whites, on verbal tests sensitive to the nondialect standard the verbal production of black children may be hampered.

Multiple Regression Analysis

The results of multiple regression analysis are similar whether TAT composite or factor scores are used as predictor variables. However, since computation of multiple correlations is facilitated by use of factor scores, only results based on such scores will be reviewed. In table 9, the multiple correlations between the six TAT factor scores and scores on the five criterion factors, age, sex, and race are presented.

By comparing the multiple correlation with the highest single correlation between predictor set and criterion set, it can be seen that substantial improvement was realized in predicting intellectual development, age, and sex.

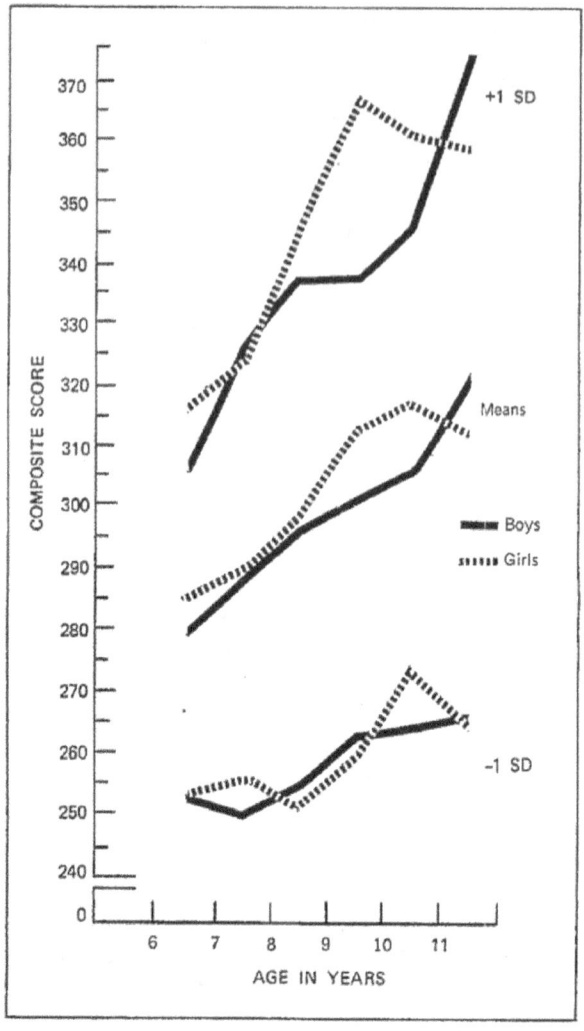

Figure 1. TAT factor 1, verbal productivity. Standard score means and scores at +1 and –1 standard deviation (SD) for boys and girls, by age.

DEVELOPMENT AND USE OF THE NATIONAL NORMS

The national probability sample was selected to represent a cross section of children ages 6-11 in the United States and initially was composed of 1,268 cases. As explained in appendix I, this number was reduced to 1,201 as a result of the loss of 67 cases with missing data or unscorable protocols. This national probability sample, drawn from the total Cycle II sample, provides a population base on which norms can be computed for the TAT scales and for projections to the total population from which the Cycle II sample was selected.

Before the norms were computed, all validity coefficients for TAT factors with criterion composites and with age and sex were recomputed for the national probability sample. TAT composite scores were computed for all children in the national probability sample and then expressed as deviation scores by age and sex groups.

Since the TAT composite norms are organized by age and sex groups, the relationships

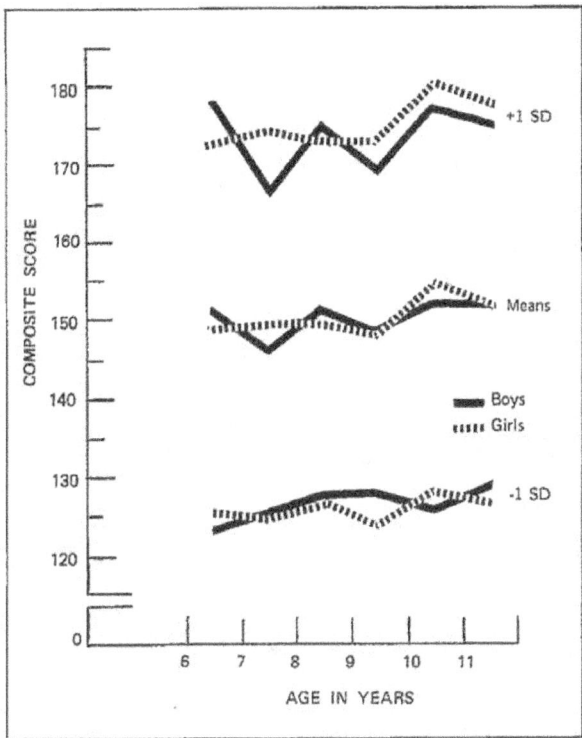

Figure 2. TAT factor II, dysphoric mood. Standard score means and scores at +1 and -1 standard deviation (SD) for boys and girls, by age.

of these composites to age and sex in the national probability sample need to be understood. All of the separate scoring manual items which define the six TAT factors (table C) were transformed to scores having a common scale (mean = 50; SD = 10) for the 1,201 subjects comprising the final sample. Composite scores were then obtained for each of the factors by summing the transformed unweighted standard scores of the items used to define each factor as listed in table C. Thus six algebraically summed scores were computed for each subject. It was decided to compute norms for composite scores only, rather than for uncorrelated factor scores. This decision reflects the fact that computation of the composites is far simpler than that for factor scores and that most applications of these scales would best be facilitated by norms based on unweighted sums.

The subjects were divided into 12 age-sex groups, and means and standard deviations of each of the six TAT composite scores were computed for each group. Table 10 presents the means

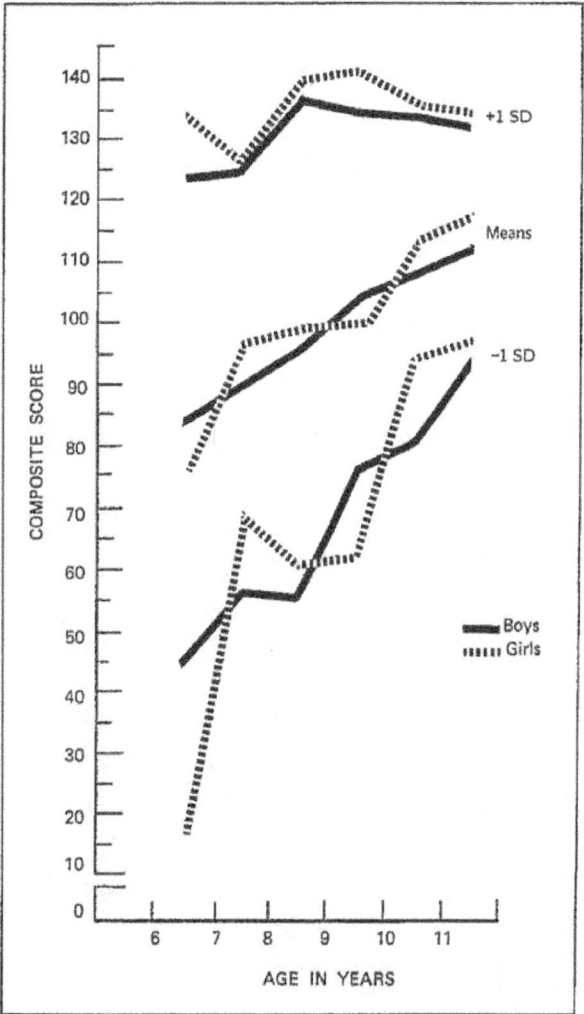

Figure 3. TAT factor III, conceptual maturity. Standard score means and scores at +1 and -1 standard deviation (SD) for boys and girls, by age.

and standard deviations at each age level for boys, for girls, and for boys and girls combined. The mean scores for each age group on the six TAT factors reported in table 10 are plotted in figures 1 through 6 for boys and for girls. In addition, the scores that would be obtained by the members of each group falling one standard deviation above or below the respective group means are shown for each TAT factor. These results provide a graphic description of the results and illustrate the growth function for each of the scales.

With the exception of the slight dip of girls' means on factors I and VI at age 11, the cognitive factors (I, III, IV, and VI) are positively and

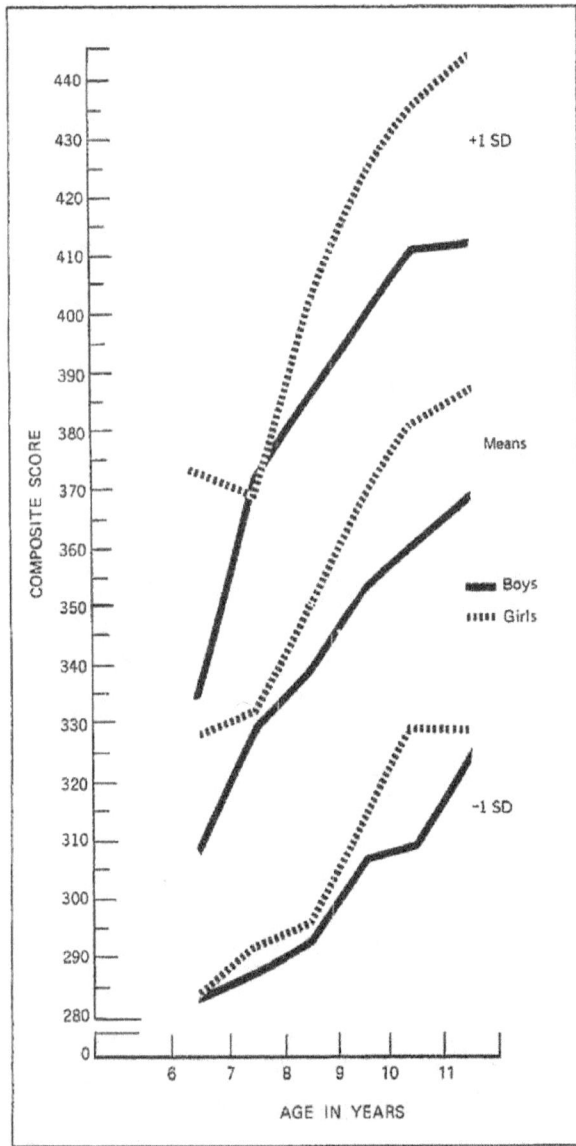

Figure 4. TAT factor IV, narrative fluency. Standard score means and scores at +1 and -1 standard deviation (SD) for boys and girls, by age.

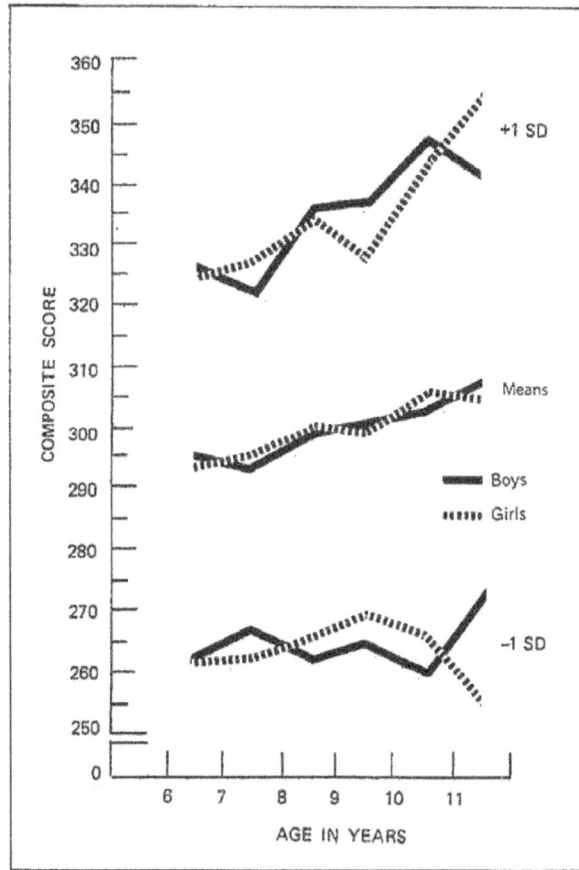

Figure 5. TAT factor V, emotionality. Standard score means and scores at +1 and -1 standard deviation (SD) for boys and girls, by age.

linearly related to age for boys and girls. Emotionality (factor V) and dysphoric mood (factor II) are essentially unrelated to age. Although the slight positive trends shown for these factors in figures 2 and 5 undoubtedly reflect growth in ability to express hostility, it seems unjustified to regard them as age-related factors. Several fluctuations in the mean scores are found in both sex groups at succeeding age levels.

Figures 1 through 6 also illustrate the overlap in the scores across the age groups on some

of the factors. The plot of the score ranges representing one standard deviation above the mean on the verbal productivity composite (figure 1) indicates that some of the boys and girls at ages 6 and 7 have scores exceeding the means of boys at ages 9 and 10. This overlap at the upper end is also true for the narrative fluency factor (figure 4) and the verbal fluency factor (figure 6).

Similarly, on the low side of the distribution, on factors III and IV (figures 3 and 4) some older subjects (ages 9-10) scoring one standard deviation below the mean of their respective groups attained scores lower than the mean score for younger age groups (ages 6-7).

Norms for the national probability sample for each of the TAT scales are presented in appendix IV. Table VII (appendix IV) contains the raw score and its standard score equivalent for each of the items from the TAT manual which are included in the six TAT factors. Total scores

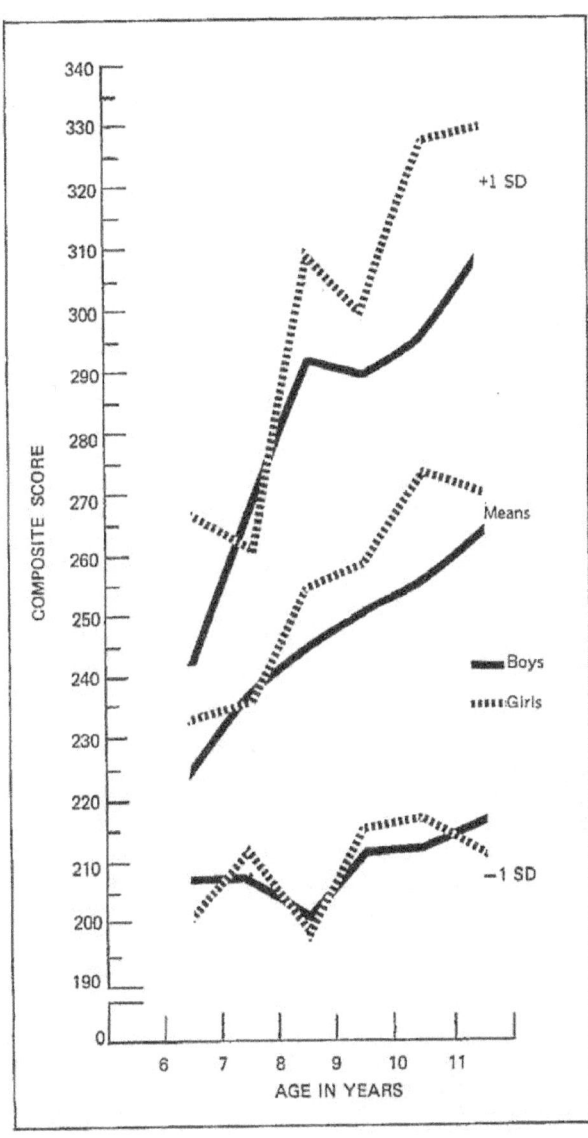

Figure 6. TAT factor VI, verbal fluency. Standard score means and scores at +1 and −1 standard deviation (SD) for boys and girls, by age.

on each of the six factors for each of the subjects in the national probability sample were obtained by summing the unweighted standard score for each of the items comprising a factor. After obtaining the total scores, frequency, cumulative frequency percentage, and cumulative percentage distributions were computed for each of the six scales. Table VIII in appendix IV constitutes the normative table for the national probability sample.

The HES five-card version of the TAT can thus be administered to any child, his scores on the scales determined, and then these can be compared with the scores of a normative sample of children of his own age and sex on each scale. For illustrative purposes, assume that a 6-year-old girl has been administered the TAT. Her performance on the verbal productivity factor (I) is obtained as follows: First, her raw scores are determined on the six items making up this scale; then by referring to the appropriate age and sex group (age 6, female) in table VII of appendix IV, the standard score equivalents for these raw scores are obtained and summed to arrive at the total composite score. Assuming that this 6-year-old girl obtains a total composite score of 300 on the verbal productivity factor, her percentile ranking in comparison to girls her age in the national probability sample is obtained from table VIII in appendix IV. In this case, the girl would have a percentile of 86. Percentile ranks in this report represent the percentage of children scoring below the raw score designated. The same procedures would be followed for all composites.

REFERENCES

[1]Sells, S. B., and Cox, S. H.: Normative studies of children's performance on the Thematic Apperception Test. I. Standardized scoring and development of measurement scales. Fort Worth. Institute of Behavioral Research, Texas Christian University, for the National Center for Health Statistics, Public Health Service. Mimeographed. Mar. 1966.

[2]Sells, S. B., and Cox, S. H.: Normative studies of children's performance on the Thematic Apperception Test. II. Test-retest reliabilities of items and scales. Fort Worth. Institute of Behavioral Research, Texas Christian University, for the National Center for Health Statistics, Public Health Service. Mimeographed. Sept. 1966.

[3]National Center for Health Statistics: Plan, operation, and response results of a program of children's examinations. *Vital and Health Statistics.* PHS Pub. No. 1000-Series 1-No. 5. Public Health Service. Washington. U.S. Government Printing Office, Oct. 1967.

[4]National Center for Health Statistics: Evaluation of psychological measures used in the Health Examination Survey of children ages 6-11. *Vital and Health Statistics.* PHS Pub. No. 1000-Series 2- No. 15. Public Health Service. Washington. U.S. Government Printing Office, Mar. 1966.

[5] Sells, S. B., Cox, S. H., and Chatham, L. R.: Scales of language development for the TAT. Proceedings, 75th Annual Convention, American Psychological Association, 1967.

[6]McNemar, Q.: *Psychological Statistics.* New York. John Wiley and Sons, 1949. pp. 60-61.

[7]Siegel, S.: *Nonparametric Statistics for the Behavioral Sciences.* New York. McGraw-Hill Book Co., 1956. pp. 229-238.

[8] Hotelling, H.: Analysis of a complex of statistical variables into principal components. *J. Educ. Psychol.* 24:417-441, 498-520, 1933.

[9]Kaiser, H. F.: The varimax criterion for analytic rotation in factor analysis. *Psychometrika* 23:187-200, 1958.

———O O O———

LIST OF SUPPLEMENTARY TABLES

Table 1. Number and percent of rejections of five TAT cards, by race, sex, and age, for the total sample ($n = 2,018$)

Race, sex, and age	Number of children in sample	Rejections of TAT cards									
		Card 1		Card 2		Card 5		Card 8 BM		Card 16	
		Number	Percent	Number	Percent	Number	Percent	Number	Percent	Number	Percent
All boys											
6-11 years-----	1,035	33	3.2	24	2.3	9	0.9	21	2.0	71	6.9
6 years-----------	172	13	7.6	9	5.2	1	0.6	5	2.9	23	13.4
7 years-----------	176	6	3.4	3	1.7	4	2.3	4	2.3	18	10.2
8 years-----------	175	7	4.0	3	1.7	3	1.7	4	2.3	9	5.1
9 years-----------	173	2	1.2	5	2.9	1	0.6	1	0.6	8	4.6
10 years----------	169	4	2.4	3	1.8	-	-	5	3.0	9	5.3
11 years----------	170	1	0.6	1	0.6	-	-	2	1.2	4	2.4
White boys[1]											
6-11 years-----	939	30	3.2	23	2.5	9	1.0	21	2.2	61	6.5
6 years-----------	155	10	6.5	9	6.0	1	0.7	5	3.3	20	13.3
7 years-----------	160	6	3.4	2	1.2	4	2.5	4	2.5	14	8.8
8 years-----------	162	7	4.3	3	1.9	3	1.9	4	2.5	8	4.9
9 years-----------	158	2	1.3	5	3.2	1	0.6	1	0.6	8	5.1
10 years----------	154	4	2.6	3	1.9	-	-	5	3.2	8	5.2
11 years----------	150	1	0.7	1	0.7	-	-	2	1.3	3	2.0
Black boys											
6-11 years-----	96	3	3.1	1	1.0	-	-	-	-	10	10.0
6 years-----------	17	3	17.6	-	-	-	-	-	-	3	17.6
7 years-----------	16	-	-	1	6.2	-	-	-	-	4	25.0
8 years-----------	13	-	-	-	-	-	-	-	-	1	7.7
9 years-----------	15	-	-	-	-	-	-	-	-	-	-
10 years----------	15	-	-	-	-	-	-	-	-	1	6.7
11 years----------	20	-	-	-	-	-	-	-	-	1	5.0
All girls											
6-11 years-----	983	40	4.1	33	3.4	17	1.7	26	2.6	66	6.7
6 years-----------	131	17	13.0	13	9.9	8	6.1	9	6.9	19	14.6
7 years-----------	164	13	7.9	6	3.7	4	2.4	1	0.6	18	11.0
8 years-----------	187	3	1.6	2	1.1	1	0.5	7	3.7	9	4.8
9 years-----------	164	4	2.4	7	4.3	3	1.8	6	3.7	14	8.5
10 years----------	169	3	1.8	5	3.0	1	1.8	3	3.0	3	3.0
11 years----------	168	-	-	-	-	-	-	-	-	3	1.8
White girls[2]											
6-11 years-----	884	35	4.0	28	3.2	13	1.5	22	2.5	52	5.9
6 years-----------	120	15	12.5	10	8.3	6	5.0	7	5.8	17	14.2
7 years-----------	145	11	7.6	6	4.1	4	2.6	1	0.7	14	9.7
8 years-----------	163	3	1.8	2	1.2	1	0.6	6	3.7	7	4.3
9 years-----------	146	3	2.1	5	3.4	1	0.7	5	3.4	10	6.8
10 years----------	157	3	1.9	5	3.2	1	0.6	3	1.9	3	1.9
11 years----------	153	-	-	-	-	-	-	-	-	1	0.7
Black girls											
6-11 years-----	99	5	5.1	5	5.1	4	4.0	4	4.0	14	14.1
6 years-----------	11	2	18.1	3	27.3	2	18.1	2	18.1	2	18.1
7 years-----------	19	2	10.5	-	-	-	-	-	-	4	21.1
8 years-----------	24	-	-	-	-	-	-	1	4.2	2	8.3
9 years-----------	18	1	5.6	2	11.1	2	11.1	1	5.6	4	22.2
10 years----------	12	-	-	-	-	-	-	-	-	-	-
11 years----------	15	-	-	-	-	-	-	-	-	2	13.3

[1]Includes one oriental 11-year-old boy.
[2]Includes one oriental 6-year-old girl.

Table 2. Differences between proportions of rejections of five TAT cards by race and sex groups for the total sample ($n = 2,018$)

Comparison groups[1] and variables	TAT card				
	1	2	5	8 BM	16
All boys-all girls:					
Difference in proportions --------------	-0.0088	-0.0104	-0.0086	-0.0063	0.0015
Standard error of difference----------	0.0081	0.0072	0.0049	0.0066	0.0109
Critical ratio-------------------------	1.10	1.44	1.76	0.95	0.14
White boys-white girls:					
Difference in proportions-------------	-0.0077	-0.0072	-0.0051	-0.0024	0.0062
Standard error of difference----------	0.0084	0.0075	0.0050	0.0069	0.0110
Critical ratio------------------------	0.92	0.96	1.02	0.35	0.56
Black boys-black girls:					
Difference in proportions-------------	-0.0193	-0.0401	-0.0401	-0.0401	-0.0373
Standard error of difference----------	0.0283	0.0246	0.0203	0.0203	0.0470
Critical ratio------------------------	-0.68	1.63	[2]1.99	[2]1.99	0.79
All white-all black:					
Difference in proportions-------------	-0.0053	-0.0028	-0.0085	-0.0031	-0.0611
Standard error of difference----------	0.0141	0.0125	0.0085	0.0114	0.0190
Critical ratio------------------------	0.38	0.22	1.00	0.27	[3]3.22
White boys-black boys:					
Difference in proportions-------------	0.0007	0.0141	0.0096	0.0224	-0.0393
Standard error of difference----------	0.0188	0.0161	0.0099	0.0151	0.0270
Critical ratio------------------------	0.04	0.88	0.97	1.48	1.46
White girls-black girls:					
Difference in proportions-------------	-0.0109	-0.0188	-0.0257	-0.0155	-0.0826
Standard error of difference----------	0.0209	0.0190	0.0138	0.0170	0.0264
Critical ratio------------------------	0.52	0.99	1.86	0.91	[3]3.13

[1]White includes one oriental 11-year-old boy and one oriental 6-year-old girl.
[2]Significant at .05 level.
[3]Significant at .01 level.

27

Table 3. Correlations[1] among the 68 criterion variables

Variable	1	2	3	4	5	6	7	8	9	10	11	12	13	14	15	16	17	18	19	20	21	22	23	24	25	26	27	28	29
1 Grade repeated																													
2 Grade skipped	25																												
3 Gifted child/slow learner	31	02																											
4 Pays attention	25	03	40																										
5 Intellectual ability	32	06	55	54																									
6 Academic performance	33	08	53	60	82																								
7 Intellectual adjustment scale	36	06	71	78	89	91																							
8 Emotionally disturbed	18	06	07	22	13	14	17																						
9 Overall adjustment	21	08	24	52	34	42	47	21																					
10 Motor activity	10	06	12	16	13	16	17	17	21																				
11 Aggression	16	13	12	28	14	17	22	35	34	21																			
12 Frequency of being chosen leader	11	04	09	31	15	18	23	09	23	03	29																		
13 Rank order when choosing sides	18	09	31	38	34	37	43	13	33	14	13	08																	
14 Frequency of disciplinary action	18	08	33	42	38	44	48	12	39	16	16	09	60																
15 Social maladjustment scale	28	14	33	56	41	48	55	40	70	45	67	46	62	65															
16 Nursery school attendance	-01	08	02	-06	-03	-01	-03	02	-03	06	01	-01	-03	03	01														
17 Special resources for physical disabilities	05	-03	06	07	09	07	09	08	04	05	05	04	02	04	07	-02													
18 Present health status	04	01	09	08	09	09	10	09	05	11	10	04	08	11	14	05	11												
19 Wets bed	05	06	08	15	09	08	12	05	04	06	07	04	10	07	11	07	-02	06											
20 Permanent scars	-01	06	-01	04	-01	02	02	04	04	03	-	03	03	03	05	-03	04	03	08										
21 Serious hospitalization	-	01	-	01	-02	02	-	11	07	01	05	06	08	02	08	02	03	04	02	-01									
22 Serious accident or injury	05	08	-01	05	03	05	04	04	07	-	07	08	04	08	-07	07	18	11	06	12									
23 Scarlet fever	02	08	-02	-	-01	02	-	-01	-	02	-01	03	-	-01	01	-02	-	08	-	02	-01	03							
24 Rheumatic fever	07	-01	-01	04	08	07	06	05	02	04	-02	01	02	-01	02	-02	04	10	01	-02	05	08	-01						
25 Polio	04	-01	-01	-	01	-	01	-01	-	-	-02	-08	01	-01	-02	-01	-01	-01	-02	-01	-01	02	-01	-03					
26 Meningitis or sleeping sickness	-01	-03	-	-	-04	-04	-03	-01	03	-02	-01	03	01	-	-	-01	-01	-01	-01	-01	09	-01	-	-					
27 Tuberculosis	-	-	-	-	-	-	-	-	-	-	-	-	-	-	-	-	-	-	-	-	-	-	-	-	-	-			
28 Diabetes	-	-	-	-	-	-	-	-	-	-	-	-	-	-	-	-	-	-	-	-	-	-	-	-	-	-	-		
29 Epilepsy	-02	-01	03	03	01	03	03	-01	03	-	-02	05	04	02	03	04	-01	-01	-02	-01	07	07	-01	-	-	-	-	-	
30 Whooping cough	07	-	04	05	03	07	08	04	05	-02	-03	-01	03	03	02	03	05	13	02	04	01	04	03	03	-02	-01	-	-	-02
31 Measles (yes, no)	06	-	10	07	11	11	12	02	07	07	05	-01	09	07	09	04	03	08	-	02	03	04	05	03	02	01	-	-	-03
32 Asthma	02	-03	01	-	02	03	02	02	-	07	01	-	-	02	06	-01	02	-06	07	11	-04	-01	-01	-	-	-01			
33 Measles (severity)	03	-03	-	-03	-01	-	-01	-	02	04	-02	-02	-03	01	-01	03	09	24	04	-06	02	15	03	10	-01	-01	-	-	-01
34 Hay fever	-04	-03	-02	-12	-07	-06	-08	-02	-05	04	-03	-04	-07	-02	-05	02	04	06	-	-04	-	03	06	04	-01	-01	-	-	-01
35 Other allergies	03	-01	-02	-	-06	-03	-01	-01	02	-01	04	03	-04	-04	-	10	-02	-06	04	11	-	07	-02	-01	-	-	-02		
36 Kidney trouble	04	16	-02	03	-	03	02	-02	06	02	11	02	05	-01	08	03	09	20	03	-	13	06	06	-01	-01	-	-	-01	
37 Heart trouble	-05	-01	-02	-	03	02	01	01	01	10	-02	04	02	03	04	-	02	06	01	01	04	-04	-02	-01	-01	-	-	-	
38 Convulsions, fits	-01	02	08	05	06	05	07	03	04	01	08	04	01	03	06	-04	02	10	-	-	09	12	02	-01	-01	-	-	17	
39 Present health problems	05	-03	04	03	04	03	05	07	03	04	04	-	03	09	07	-03	07	35	11	05	08	18	07	04	-03	07	-	-	07
40 Speech defect	04	02	-	-01	-	01	-	02	-01	01	-01	-03	02	07	01	05	02	11	13	04	02	06	-04	-02	-11	-01	-	-	-01
41 Hearing difficulty	04	-03	02	02	05	03	03	02	01	01	03	06	01	05	03	-	33	05	07	01	07	06	-03	03	-02	-01	-	-	-02
42 Suck thumb, fingers	-06	-01	-01	01	-02	-02	-01	01	02	-01	02	01	03	-01	01	-07	04	05	06	01	-	-02	-06	02	10	-	-	-02	
43 Prevented from strenuous exercise	04	08	-	-02	-01	04	-	09	-	01	-01	05	03	-	02	07	-	25	07	07	-	19	01	16	-01	-01	-	-	14
44 Unpleasant dreams	04	05	-02	03	-01	04	02	01	03	-06	-02	01	-	01	-	04	-03	-03	-02	-03	01	-03	03	-01	-05	-	-	-01	
45 Sleepwalking	02	08	-03	01	-02	01	-01	01	04	-01	01	04	07	-05	-07	-	06	-01	03	08	-01	02	04	-	-01	-	-	-02	
46 Fear of dark	04	-06	07	06	09	10	10	06	10	-02	-02	04	05	06	06	01	05	10	08	01	05	10	13	06	01	-02	-	-	-03
47 Medical history scale	10	04	07	10	09	13	12	12	11	08	07	08	03	09	15	02	28	48	34	16	22	46	15	16	-	02	-	-	06
48 Residence location	-01	04	-02	01	01	02	01	02	-07	-04	01	02	03	-02	03	01	-05	06	07	03	05	05	05	-01	02	-08	02	-	-
49 Income level	-15	-04	-13	-11	-18	-15	-17	-04	-04	-02	-07	02	-08	-11	-09	-	-07	-10	-10	-02	02	-03	-01	-02	03	02	-	-	-
50 Foreign language	01	-01	02	-02	05	05	03	-06	03	-02	02	01	-03	01	-	01	-03	04	02	02	-	-03	-06	-02	-02	-01	-	-	04
51 Range of food tastes	-04	-06	-02	-06	-02	-04	-05	-	-	-02	-02	-07	-01	-01	-04	-03	04	05	05	-05	05	01	-01	-05	-03	-02	-	-	01
52 New friends	02	01	06	02	04	03	04	-05	-	01	-06	07	-	04	05	02	-01	05	05	02	-01	03	-03	-03	-01	-	-	-03	
53 Interchild relations	05	01	05	14	10	12	13	07	13	02	08	05	11	14	15	-03	01	04	05	04	08	08	06	-	04	02	-	-	-02
54 Run away from home	-01	04	04	04	05	06	06	03	05	-03	-	04	03	04	03	06	-04	-04	05	03	06	07	01	-01	-01	-	-	-01
55 Trauma	07	35	04	03	04	04	02	05	-	01	04	05	07	05	04	06	07	10	01	09	-	01							
56 Tension level	07	05	02	07	07	09	08	14	09	03	09	03	07	07	12	-07	08	09	13	05	09	10	02	05	-02	07	-	-	-02
57 Temper	04	09	06	11	10	12	12	11	14	-	13	05	08	07	15	-06	02	07	15	04	11	09	-02	-03	07	-01	-	-	-02
58 School social adjustment scale	07	04	08	10	11	12	13	08	13	01	05	-03	08	12	11	-06	06	11	15	07	10	10	01	02	02	-	-	-03	
59 WRAT Reading score	-22	-04	-29	-25	-33	-31	-36	-13	06	13	-04	-07	-08	-12	-15	-17	18	-06	04	-05	-14	-10	-14	01	-01	05	-	-	05
60 WRAT Arithmetic score	-07	09	-08	-09	-08	-11	-11	-	11	-	01	-05	-06	-02	-06	18	-05	04	-08	-05	02	-04	04	-01	-	-01	-	-	-04
61 Age in months	07	07	-01	-05	02	03	-	02	03	-	03	-05	-	01	-	07	-09	01	-10	-02	-02	03	05	-01	09	-01	-	-	04
62 Sex	-08	-04	-05	-20	-11	-13	75	01	09	18	-03	-18	-22	-01	-02	-18	-	-03	-03	-04	-02	-	-05	03	-02	-01	03	-	-	02
63 Race	09	-01	05	07	10	08	09	01	07	02	04	-01	02	04	04	-11	03	11	04	09	01	04	-05	-02	-02	-01	-	-	-02
64 Sample number	-	-	-	-	-	-	-	-	-	-	-	-	-	-	-	-	-	-	-	-	-	-	-	-	-	-	-	-	-
65 Manually recorded protocol	-01	-02	-01	-01	-01	-02	-01	-	02	-02	02	-01	03	-03	-08	-03	-03	03	01	03	01	03	-01	-01	-03	-01	-	-	-01
66 Goodenough-Harris score	-12	01	-22	-23	-24	-23	-27	-06	-12	-06	-03	-11	-10	-10	-14	06	-16	-03	-15	-03	-05	-	-04	03	-02	06	03	-	-	03
67 WISC Vocabulary raw score	-17	-	-26	-22	-33	-28	-33	-02	-10	-02	-04	-02	-12	-15	-12	09	-13	-11	-11	-04	-	-01	09	-04	07	01	-	-	02
68 WISC Block Design raw score	-14	-04	-20	-23	-29	-28	-31	-08	-17	-06	-05	-07	-10	-14	-16	02	-10	-06	-01	-05	-02	-02	-	-	06	02	-	-	-02

[1]Decimal points have been omitted because of space limitation.

Variable—Con.

Row	30	31	32	33	34	35	36	37	38	39	40	41	42	43	44	45	46	47	48	49	50	51	52	53	54	55	56	57	58	59	60	61	62	63	64	65	66	67
31	03																																					
32	08	09																																				
33	02	06	02																																			
34	-07	-02	-02	25																																		
35	-07	02	01	16	17																																	
36	02	02	08	06	03	10																																
37	-04	-05	01	-04	-	-02	-03																															
38	-01	-02	02	07	01	04	01	09																														
39	05	09	05	21	11	15	07	01	11																													
40	-02	06	02	04	02	-01	11	04	-02	19																												
41	02	03	02	01	-03	-01	-	-04	03	10	09																											
42	-03	01	-	01	-05	08	03	02	04	01	02	02																										
43	-	05	-	21	11	12	11	03	10	21	03	10	06																									
44	06	02	05	04	04	01	02	-02	-02	-01	06	-	02	01																								
45	-	02	03	02	04	06	06	03	06	03	13	06	02	04	27																							
46	08	-	03	05	-	08	03	02	-	10	02	09	-05	05	06	01																						
47	21	27	23	38	24	30	30	08	23	54	28	30	19	40	13	29	37																					
48	-03	02	-03	-02	01	-03	-06	01	03	-03	-02	-	-	-06	-11	-04	-04																					
49	-17	-01	-04	02	05	03	-09	02	-03	-10	-07	-06	04	-01	04	-01	-09	-12	15																			
50	01	-07	06	02	-01	-04	-05	-	01	05	05	-03	-03	01	-04	-	02	-01	04	-12																		
51	-01	-01	02	01	01	06	-04	-	02	06	-02	05	-04	01	06	04	12	08	01	06	02																	
52	-01	-	-	01	01	02	-02	03	01	-01	-02	06	04	01	02	-	03	04	01																			
53	-01	03	05	-02	01	07	04	04	05	06	-05	04	-01	04	-01	-04	07	10	01	-04	02	03	18															
54	03	06	03	04	04	-03	04	-02	07	01	09	-02	-01	06	04	06	03	08	07	01	-03	-02	-02	02														
55	-02	03	01	08	02	10	08	01	09	12	07	04	02	10	-01	04	17	01	-06	-02	-	06	05															
56	-	06	02	01	04	05	09	-02	03	12	02	04	01	05	-	04	07	19	01	-03	-04	07	02	15	06	17												
57	06	02	09	-05	-04	-03	04	02	03	06	03	-	-01	-	11	02	05	12	-	-10	06	04	-	16	07	02	29											
58	-	04	06	02	-	09	05	-	08	12	01	09	01	08	02	03	07	21	02	-02	02	33	60	60	14	37	48	42										
59	-04	07	-03	04	09	03	-05	02	01	-04	-04	-16	-05	02	-06	03	-09	-08	03	22	-04	02	-04	-07	-03	03	01	-06	-05									
60	-02	02	-03	03	06	-02	-01	-03	01	-02	-02	-10	-07	-05	01	-02	-03	-07	03	08	-02	-03	-03	-06	-	-02	-02	-02	-07	86								
61	07	15	-02	07	06	01	-01	-	04	03	-02	-13	-11	06	-02	06	-07	01	-	-	-02	-02	-03	-04	-	03	02	06	-01	69	79							
62	-02	-03	-04	01	-01	02	-	-07	-03	-06	-05	09	-01	-05	-05	01	-06	-03	03	03	-03	-01	03	02	-03	-10	-03	-04	-12	-05	15	08	03					
63	14	04	-02	-	-04	-05	03	-02	-02	09	03	07	03	01	-04	-04	05	09	08	-26	-08	02	-02	-02	-03	-05	-05	04	-03	-18	-15	01	01					
64	-	-	-	-	-	-	-	-	-	-	-	-	-	-	-	-	-	-	-	-	-	-	-	-	-	-	-	-	-	-	-	-02	-	-05	-			
65	04	03	05	01	-02	01	-	-02	-	-04	-03	-02	01	01	03	05	-03	02	-06	06	-03	04	04	-01	02	01	-03	01	03	-	-	-02	-	-05	-			
66	-05	05	01	-	05	02	-03	-05	-02	-04	-03	-11	-06	-02	-03	05	-08	-10	-04	10	-01	-05	-05	-12	-04	-04	-07	-06	-14	63	64	56	17	-14	-	02		
67	-08	06	-02	01	09	09	-04	03	-	-04	-04	-14	-08	01	-	09	-09	-07	02	24	-11	-	-07	-07	01	03	01	-06	-07	77	75	62	-	-26	-	-	59	
69	-07	03	01	03	05	02	-03	-02	-03	-	03	-11	-06	02	01	03	-11	-08	-05	21	-	-02	-	-09	-03	-02	-05	-06	-08	57	61	50	-02	-22	-	-	02	57	61

29

Table 4. Varimax rotated loadings of 64 criterion variables selected from HES Cycle II questionnaires and tests on five principal components ($n=2,012$)[1]

Variable	Rotated factor				
	I	II	III	IV	V
1. Grade repeated	.43	-.08	.08	-	-.12
2. Grade skipped	.06	-.02	-.04	.02	-.22
3. Gifted child/slow learner	.71	-.01	.12	.02	.02
4. Pays attention	.66	.04	.13	.03	-.37
5. Intellectual ability	.85	-.05	.15	.05	-.02
6. Academic performance	.86	-.04	.12	.04	-.11
8. Emotionally disturbed	.09	-.05	.03	.04	-.49
9. Overall adjustment	.43	.03	.05	.07	-.54
10. Motor activity	.15	-.04	-	-.07	-.36
11. Aggression	.10	.03	-	-.02	-.71
12. Frequency of being chosen leader	.50	-.10	-.09	.02	.13
13. Rank order when choosing sides	.51	-	-	.05	-.30
14. Frequency of disciplinary action	.56	-	-	.06	-.28
16. Nursery school or kindergarten attendance	.01	-.05	-.10	-.12	-.02
17. Special resources for physical disabilities	.03	-.20	.22	.01	-.05
18. Present health status	.10	-.54	.08	.01	-.06
19. Wets bed	.04	-.23	.19	.16	-.13
20. Permanent scars	-.02	-.08	.09	.08	-.10
21. Serious hospitalization	-.05	-.14	.01	.14	-.18
22. Serious accident or injury	-.02	-.44	.03	.08	-.14
23. Scarlet fever	.02	-.13	-.08	-	-
24. Rheumatic fever	.10	-.17	-.06	-.02	-.03
25. Polio	.05	.01	-.11	.06	.05
26. Meningitis or sleeping sickness	-.03	-.01	-	.02	-.02
27. Tuberculosis	-	-	-	-	-
28. Diabetes	-	-	-	-	-
29. Epilepsy	.04	-.07	-.03	-.05	-.02
30. Whooping cough	.14	-.18	.07	-.04	.09
31. Measles (yes, no)	.20	-.23	-.15	.01	-
32. Asthma	.01	-.19	.03	.07	-
33. Measles (severity)	.01	-.48	-.04	-.06	.06
34. Hay fever	-.07	-.29	-.09	-.02	.06
35. Other allergies	-.06	-.31	-.05	.08	-.03
36. Kidney trouble	-.05	-.28	.07	.02	-.15
37. Heart trouble	-.01	-.02	.02	-	-.06
38. Convulsions, fits	.04	-.20	-.02	.08	-.09
39. Present health problems	.03	-.58	.05	.06	-.02
40. Speech defect	-.01	-.28	.07	-.04	-.02
41. Hearing difficulty	-.01	-.23	.26	.06	-
42. Suck thumb, fingers	-.07	-.08	.15	.01	-.04
43. Prevented from strenuous exercise, health defects	.15	-.17	.08	-.06	.19
44. Unpleasant dreams	.01	-.17	.03	-.17	-.02
45. Sleepwalking[2]	-.40	-.13	.09	-.07	-.62
46. Fear of dark	.11	-.28	.13	.05	.03
48. Residence location[3]	-.40	.61	-.16	.61	-.85
49. Income level	-.23	.17	-.21	.06	-.07
50. Foreign language	.06	.01	.05	.03	.07
51. Range of food tastes	-.05	-.06	.02	.31	.07
52. New friends	.08	.04	.02	.53	.18
53. Interchild relations	.11	-	.04	.60	-.08
54. Run away from home	.02	-.07	-	.14	-.08
55. Trauma	.01	-.19	-.03	.32	-.06
56. Tension level	.02	-.13	-.01	.52	-.19
57. Temper	.07	-.03	.02	.47	-.18
59. WRAT Reading score	-.24	-.02	-.79	-	.04
60. WRAT Arithmetic score	-.04	-	-.80	-.07	-
61. Age in months	.16	-.13	-.82	-.01	.05
62. Sex	-.05	.01	-.04	-.01	.31
63. Race	.13	-.11	.24	-.09	.06
64. Sample number	-	-	-	-	-
65. Handwritten protocol	-.03	-	-	.05	.03
66. Goodenough-Harris score	-.13	-.01	-.73	-.11	.08
67. WISC Vocabulary raw score	-.24	-.02	-.82	-.01	-.05
68. WISC Block Design raw score	-.21	.02	-.71	.07	.05

[1] The variables used to define each factor are listed in table A and are discussed on pp. 9-11.
[2] This variable was dropped due to insufficient variance.
[3] This variable was dropped due to error in definition.

NOTE: Four criterion scales from Study I—variables 7, 15, 47, and 58—were omitted from this analysis.

Table 5. Means and standard deviations (SD) of 68 criterion variables selected from HES Cycle II questionnaires and tests grouped by factors, by sex and age (n = 2,012)

Criterion factor and variable[1]	Boys 6 and 7 years Mean	SD	Boys 8 and 9 years Mean	SD	Boys 10 and 11 years Mean	SD	Girls 6 and 7 years Mean	SD	Girls 8 and 9 years Mean	SD	Girls 10 and 11 years Mean	SD
Factor I—School adjustment												
1 Grade repeated	0.065	0.240	0.170	0.380	0.175	0.375	0.070	0.250	0.105	0.300	0.070	0.260
3 Gifted child/slow learner	1.080	0.395	1.125	0.480	1.085	0.535	1.030	0.470	1.035	0.450	1.015	0.445
4 Pays attention	1.080	0.630	1.165	0.655	1.095	0.630	0.890	0.610	0.855	0.630	0.850	0.645
5 Intellectual ability	0.950	0.615	0.965	0.655	0.995	0.685	0.825	0.645	0.815	0.635	0.865	0.625
6 Academic performance	1.010	0.665	1.055	0.695	1.080	0.685	0.865	0.665	0.830	0.675	0.890	0.650
Factor II—Poor health												
18 Present health status	0.035	0.185	0.055	0.230	0.055	0.230	0.050	0.220	0.055	0.220	0.040	0.195
22 Serious accident or injury	0.190	0.390	0.220	0.415	0.195	0.395	0.135	0.340	0.155	0.365	0.170	0.375
33 Measles (severity)	0.030	0.195	0.070	0.245	0.070	0.245	0.050	0.230	0.035	0.190	0.075	0.270
34 Hay fever	0.050	0.215	0.055	0.225	0.075	0.260	0.040	0.190	0.040	0.190	0.060	0.240
35 Other allergies	0.135	0.340	0.145	0.355	0.090	0.285	0.085	0.275	0.125	0.325	0.130	0.340
36 Kidney trouble	0.030	0.170	0.025	0.155	0.025	0.165	0.040	0.195	0.050	0.220	0.060	0.230
39 Present health problems	0.170	0.380	0.180	0.390	0.200	0.400	0.165	0.375	0.155	0.360	0.190	0.395
40 Speech defect	0.045	0.205	0.045	0.210	0.035	0.190	0.030	0.160	0.020	0.150	0.040	0.190
Factor III—Intellectual development												
59 WRAT Reading score	31.550	14.745	51.880	15.485	63.290	15.485	36.090	13.930	57.690	13.010	67.780	13.315
60 WRAT Arithmetic score	19.115	5.630	27.140	5.080	34.180	6.800	19.880	4.690	27.770	4.440	35.510	6.310
61 Age in months	83.235	6.930	107.840	6.960	131.850	7.210	84.835	6.510	106.950	6.680	131.660	7.220
66 Goodenough-Harris score	16.810	5.840	22.525	6.180	27.010	7.530	19.310	5.670	25.090	6.860	28.875	6.180
67 WISC Vocabulary raw score	18.160	6.085	26.390	8.110	32.405	9.095	18.100	5.645	25.335	8.935	32.500	8.520
68 WISC Block Design raw score	7.250	6.030	12.110	7.930	19.860	12.360	6.860	4.745	11.700	8.790	18.900	12.210
Factor IV—Social adjustment												
51 Range of food tastes	0.245	0.430	0.230	0.420	0.215	0.410	0.265	0.440	0.195	0.395	0.220	0.410
52 New friends	0.795	0.770	0.705	0.735	0.680	0.730	0.785	0.800	0.735	0.775	0.790	0.750
53 Interchild relations	0.615	0.565	0.620	0.575	0.605	0.570	0.535	0.560	0.520	0.570	0.520	0.570
55 Trauma	0.255	0.435	0.250	0.430	0.285	0.450	0.180	0.385	0.265	0.440	0.260	0.440
56 Tension level	0.135	0.345	0.205	0.400	0.195	0.395	0.130	0.335	0.140	0.345	0.150	0.355
57 Temper	0.175	0.385	0.225	0.420	0.195	0.400	0.115	0.320	0.100	0.300	0.150	0.360
Factor V—Emotional disturbance												
8 Emotionally disturbed	0.030	0.165	0.090	0.280	0.040	0.200	0.030	0.170	0.030	0.170	0.050	0.215
9 Overall adjustment	1.025	0.570	1.135	0.550	1.070	0.575	0.890	0.475	0.880	0.520	0.870	0.560
10 Motor activity	0.285	0.455	0.355	0.480	0.325	0.470	0.250	0.475	0.295	0.455	0.285	0.455
11 Aggression	0.340	0.860	0.490	1.045	0.380	0.915	0.065	0.290	0.140	0.490	0.130	0.440
Miscellaneous variables												
2 Grade skipped	0.010	0.110	0.020	0.140	0.020	0.150	0.005	0.040	0.015	0.130	0.010	0.095
7 Intellectual adjustment scale	4.115	1.855	4.310	2.090	4.250	2.115	3.620	2.020	3.530	2.015	3.630	1.935
12 Frequency of being chosen leader	0.630	0.485	0.695	0.465	0.645	0.475	0.465	0.505	0.390	0.490	0.410	0.490
13 Rank order when choosing sides	0.865	0.555	0.885	0.580	0.830	0.575	0.795	0.570	0.820	0.625	0.820	0.590
14 Frequency of disciplinary action	1.090	0.515	1.055	0.615	1.110	0.615	1.040	0.510	1.050	0.610	1.060	0.600
15 Social maladjustment scale	4.270	2.215	4.700	2.485	4.415	2.370	3.535	1.705	3.600	1.895	3.635	1.845
16 Nursery school or kindergarten attendance	0.070	0.250	0.085	0.280	0.105	0.300	0.070	0.255	0.095	0.295	0.115	0.315
17 Special resources for physical disabilities	0.095	0.290	0.080	0.270	0.060	0.240	0.090	0.280	0.055	0.230	0.035	0.185
19 Wets bed	0.180	0.385	0.200	0.400	0.130	0.340	0.150	0.360	0.090	0.285	0.085	0.280
20 Permanent scars	0.050	0.215	0.040	0.180	0.035	0.190	0.045	0.205	0.040	0.195	0.045	0.210
21 Serious hospitalization	0.035	0.190	0.055	0.225	0.035	0.190	0.040	0.195	0.045	0.205	0.040	0.200
23 Scarlet fever	0.020	0.130	0.025	0.155	0.040	0.195	0.020	0.140	0.045	0.200	0.045	0.210
24 Rheumatic fever	-	-	-	-	-	0.080	0.005	0.080	0.005	0.040	0.005	0.040
25 Polio	-	-	-	-	0.010	0.090	0.005	0.040	-	0.040	0.005	0.040
26 Meningitis or sleeping sickness	-	0.040	-	0.040	-	-	-	-	0.010	0.095	0.005	0.040
27 Tuberculosis	-	-	-	0.040	-	-	-	-	-	-	-	-
28 Diabetes	-	-	-	-	-	0.040	-	-	-	-	-	-
29 Epilepsy	-	0.040	-	-	-	0.040	-	-	-	0.040	0.010	0.095
30 Whooping cough	0.075	0.255	0.080	0.270	0.100	0.300	0.040	0.190	0.070	0.255	0.090	0.285
31 Measles (yes, no)	0.765	0.425	0.890	0.305	0.905	0.290	0.750	0.430	0.865	0.340	0.910	0.285
32 Asthma	0.030	0.175	0.035	0.175	0.040	0.200	0.055	0.225	0.065	0.240	0.050	0.220
37 Heart trouble	0.030	0.170	0.025	0.155	0.020	0.130	0.010	0.095	0.015	0.120	0.015	0.115
38 Convulsions, fits	0.040	0.200	0.050	0.220	0.050	0.215	0.030	0.160	0.025	0.155	0.040	0.190
41 Hearing difficulty	0.145	0.355	0.080	0.270	0.070	0.245	0.090	0.285	0.055	0.225	0.055	0.225
42 Suck thumb, fingers	0.080	0.275	0.060	0.230	0.060	0.245	0.190	0.390	0.120	0.325	0.070	0.255
43 Prevented from strenuous exercise, health defects	0.055	0.230	0.040	0.195	0.075	0.270	0.050	0.220	0.050	0.220	0.070	0.260
44 Unpleasant dreams	0.030	0.165	0.025	0.150	0.010	0.105	0.015	0.130	0.015	0.085	0.010	0.105
45 Sleepwalking	0.070	0.260	0.105	0.300	0.130	0.335	0.075	0.255	0.075	0.270	0.110	0.310
46 Fear of dark	0.270	0.445	0.235	0.420	0.135	0.340	0.250	0.430	0.250	0.430	0.205	0.400
47 Medical history scale	2.685	1.875	2.835	1.930	2.695	1.900	2.510	1.790	2.540	1.645	2.675	1.845
48 Residence location	1.710	0.450	1.680	0.465	1.705	0.455	1.635	0.485	1.700	0.460	1.680	0.475
49 Income level	5.520	2.420	5.380	2.485	5.515	2.390	5.545	2.285	5.490	2.265	5.720	2.325
50 Foreign language	0.115	0.320	0.095	0.290	0.085	0.275	0.080	0.275	0.090	0.280	0.095	0.290
54 Run away from home	0.025	0.155	0.040	0.195	0.025	0.150	0.015	0.110	0.015	0.130	0.020	0.130
58 School social adjustment scale	2.250	1.440	2.280	1.470	2.200	1.510	2.025	1.410	1.975	1.410	2.115	1.580
62 Sex	1.000	-	1.000	-	1.000	-	2.000	-	2.000	-	2.000	-
63 Race	1.095	0.295	1.080	0.270	1.100	0.305	1.100	0.300	1.120	0.325	1.080	0.270
64 Sample number	1.500	-	1.500	-	1.500	-	1.500	-	1.500	-	1.500	-
65 Handwritten protocol	0.020	0.150	0.030	0.165	0.020	0.130	0.025	0.150	0.015	0.130	0.035	0.180

[1] The original numbers assigned to the variables have been retained, even though they appear out of numerical order for this grouping by factors.

Table 6. Means and standard deviations (SD) of selected variables used in analysis of the TAT structural and thematic data ($n = 1,910$)

Variable[1]	Mean	SD
1. Adverbs	2.958	4.687
2. Pauses	15.251	17.416
3. Verbatim repetitions	5.765	8.174
4. Corrections	3.487	5.899
5. Past reference	1.264	1.561
6. Future reference	1.586	1.700
7. Unhappy outcome	0.414	0.755
8. Death	0.441	0.732
9. Murder-killing	0.271	0.555
10. Rejection	0.164	0.549
11. Level of interpretation	11.442	2.307
12. Situation complexity	11.429	2.444
13. Present reference	4.781	0.646
14. Happy outcome	1.054	1.356
15. Causally connected statements	1.239	1.395
16. Expression of feeling	2.228	1.557
17. Outcome	1.915	1.760
18. Kind-loving	0.280	0.643
19. Happy-glad	0.370	0.759
20. Goal behavior	2.659	1.840
21. Antagonism	0.119	0.437
22. Morbid mood quality	0.134	0.504
23. Bizarre theme	0.059	0.273
24. Egocentrism	0.256	0.549
25. Mean-rejecting	0.311	0.644
26. Aggression	0.506	0.732
27. Possessive adjectives	7.967	9.040
28. Common nouns	49.748	39.390
29. Pronouns	40.808	38.611
30. Single verbs	51.047	42.729
31. Dialogue	2.874	6.761
32. Age (years)[2]	8.517	1.681
33. Sex[2]	1.481	0.499
34. Race[2]	0.726	0.784
35. Criterion factor I[2]	301.275	46.879
36. Criterion factor II[2]	449.953	45.251
37. Criterion factor III[2]	300.893	45.708
38. Criterion factor IV[2]	349.828	39.090
39. Criterion factor V[2]	250.123	34.892
Purposefully connected statements[3]	0.588	0.943
Interpolations[3]	0.334	1.311
Reaction time latency[3]	60.345	62.595
Total time[3]	509.349	215.108
Number of words[3]	370.722	319.960
Thinking[3]	1.183	1.312
Escape[3]	0.091	0.322
Fear[3]	0.101	0.319
Illness-injury[3]	0.700	0.686
Number interpolated words[3]	8.128	12.103

[1] See pages 12-16 for discussion of these variables.
[2] Variable used in validation analyses.
[3] Variable not included in second phase of analysis. These are reported for possible use as resource information.

Table 7. Correlations[1] among the 31 TAT variables used in final

Variable	1	2	3	4	5	6	7	8	9	10	11	12	13	14	15	16	17	18
1 Adverbs																		
2 Pauses	47																	
3 Verbatim repetitions	35	54																
4 Corrections	51	58	52															
5 Past reference	48	44	35	60														
6 Future reference	51	51	37	56	64													
7 Unhappy outcome	12	15	13	20	19	23												
8 Death	13	15	19	21	15	16	38											
9 Murder-killing	08	11	13	15	08	07	28	76										
10 Rejection	-15	-19	-15	-14	-17	-21	-12	-11	-06									
11 Level of interpretation	34	34	35	30	36	39	30	18	09	-66								
12 Situation complexity	42	44	42	40	53	62	29	22	12	-64	80							
13 Present reference	15	20	17	15	17	22	12	10	05	-87	68	66						
14 Happy outcome	35	30	31	26	34	50	-	03	-04	-19	54	59	20					
15 Causally connected statements	34	27	33	26	29	30	28	20	10	-20	72	52	22	50				
16 Expression of feeling	40	27	27	31	41	41	21	12	04	-30	56	52	32	43	50			
17 Outcome	41	38	36	38	45	64	44	22	10	-25	63	71	27	78	56	47		
18 Kind-loving	16	19	20	11	15	19	02	02	-	-11	31	31	12	34	32	26	29	
19 Happy-glad	30	21	26	20	29	31	-	05	-02	-12	28	33	13	45	27	43	34	29
20 Goal behavior	24	23	28	18	25	30	15	10	06	-29	50	48	32	39	41	41	42	39
21 Antagonism	15	14	18	16	15	17	14	10	10	-06	19	20	06	16	23	21	19	25
22 Morbid mood quality	12	13	23	20	13	15	04	09	10	-05	10	15	06	10	10	10	11	12
23 Bizarre theme	07	07	07	07	10	05	13	32	30	-04	06	10	04	-	07	07	08	13
24 Egocentrism	21	22	19	24	24	27	16	12	14	-11	24	28	12	16	22	22	29	12
25 Mean-rejecting	21	17	20	21	18	18	21	19	19	-10	23	24	08	13	28	29	24	22
26 Aggression	04	13	15	10	08	07	16	26	33	-11	13	16	11	01	10	06	09	11
27 Possessive adjectives	52	46	43	49	50	48	22	22	14	-20	51	59	22	46	54	47	54	36
28 Common nouns	57	54	53	51	48	49	20	27	19	-27	56	65	28	50	57	45	57	35
29 Pronouns	61	54	56	56	51	53	23	27	19	-24	58	66	26	52	60	52	60	36
30 Single verbs	63	55	55	56	51	53	22	26	17	-26	57	66	28	51	58	51	59	35
31 Dialogue	33	24	30	27	27	28	12	14	13	-09	27	34	10	27	30	26	32	22
32 Age	30	20	14	15	30	28	11	-	-05	-16	36	36	18	34	32	36	36	17
33 Sex	03	-01	-04	-	04	02	01	-03	-06	03	03	05	02	-03	06	13	11	05	02
34 Race	16	20	07	25	26	32	01	-	-	-	-05	11	01	-	-09	-	06	-06
35 Criterion factor I	14	09	05	09	17	18	06	-01	-05	-03	15	17	05	20	17	14	20	07
36 Criterion factor II	-	-03	-02	-01	-	-	-	-01	-01	02	-02	-01	-01	02	-03	-01	01	02
37 Criterion factor III	42	31	18	24	45	44	13	-	-06	-18	42	48	23	42	36	42	45	21
38 Criterion factor IV	03	05	02	-	03	05	-02	-	-	-	03	05	-	07	02	02	05	04
39 Criterion factor V	-02	-03	-01	-	-02	-02	-	02	04	-	-06	-05	-01	-10	-08	-02	-08	-05

[1]Decimal points have been omitted because of space limitation.
[2]See pages 12-16 for discussion of the 31 TAT variables and pages 9-11 for discussion of the five criterion factors.

analysis, five criterion factors, age, sex, and race[2] (*n* = 1,910)

	19	20	21	22	23	24	25	26	27	28	29	30	31	32	33	34	35	36	37	38	
																					1
																					2
																					3
																					4
																					5
																					6
																					7
																					8
																					9
																					10
																					11
																					12
																					13
																					14
																					15
																					16
																					17
																					18
																					19
	24																				20
	11	29																			21
	09	19	22																		22
	04	19	19	10																	23
	09	22	21	13	23																24
	12	32	42	10	34	30															25
	01	29	20	15	33	17	31														26
	35	35	30	21	14	30	32	11													27
	37	39	28	21	17	31	34	19	84												28
	38	44	29	23	17	34	37	17	80	89											29
	39	42	28	23	16	33	35	17	82	93	96										30
	24	21	21	09	12	17	23	11	52	53	54	56									31
	14	31	13	-	01	12	09	-	30	32	32	32	06								32
	08	-08	-05	-07	-06	-04	-	-13	11	04	07	06	04	02							33
	04	-07	-01	-	-	02	-01	-03	09	09	06	08	-	01	-						34
	12	11	-	-	-03	04	02	-03	17	16	17	18	05	-03	16	06					35
	-	-	01	-01	-	-02	09	-02	-	-	-01	-01	-02	04	-03	03	-04				36
	22	35	12	-	02	14	09	-02	38	40	41	42	09	77	02	14	27	02			37
	03	02	-03	-02	04	03	-	-	05	05	05	05	01	-01	08	06	11	-20	03		38
	-03	-03	-	01	02	-01	-	05	-05	-04	-06	-05	-	02	-19	06	-43	08	-09	-12	39

Table 8. Varimax rotated loadings of 31 TAT variables on six principal components $(n = 1,910)$[1]

Variable	Rotated factor					
	I	II	III	IV	V	VI
1. Adverbs	.57	.01	.03	.22	-.03	.38
2. Pauses	.69	.03	.14	.05	-.10	.28
3. Verbatim repetitions	.50	.04	.13	.04	-.16	.42
4. Corrections	.80	.10	.05	.04	-.09	.22
5. Past reference	.72	.05	.06	.29	-.08	.08
6. Future reference	.73	.05	.08	.43	-.07	.03
7. Unhappy outcome	.17	.60	.03	.35	-.10	-.16
8. Death	.08	.85	.05	-	-.11	.17
9. Murder-killing	.02	.82	.03	-.12	-.18	.16
10. Rejection	-.08	-.03	-.93	-.10	.04	-.04
11. Level of interpretation	.15	.11	.65	.57	-.09	.25
12. Situation complexity	.39	.11	.59	.51	-.11	.23
13. Present reference	.09	.02	.93	.12	-.04	.04
14. Happy outcome	.21	-.11	.09	.73	-	.25
15. Causally connected statements	.05	.16	.15	.64	-.11	.39
16. Expression of feeling	.23	.01	.22	.57	-.15	.20
17. Outcome	.37	.19	.13	.78	-.06	.12
18. Kind-loving	-.08	-.17	.05	.38	-.35	.35
19. Happy-glad	.15	-.13	.01	.43	-.03	.31
20. Goal behavior	.06	-.05	.29	.43	-.49	.15
21. Antagonism	.06	-.04	-.04	.18	-.63	.12
22. Morbid mood quality	.23	-.07	.05	-.09	-.39	.14
23. Bizarre theme	-	.32	-	-.05	-.57	.05
24. Egocentrism	.30	.08	.03	.18	-.44	-.01
25. Mean-rejecting	.07	.13	-.01	.19	-.66	.14
26. Aggression	.01	.28	.14	-.09	-.58	.04
27. Possessive adjectives	.38	.09	.09	.36	-.17	.65
28. Common nouns	.41	.12	.17	.31	-.19	.71
29. Pronouns	.45	.12	.14	.37	-.21	.67
30. Single verbs	.45	.11	.16	.34	-.19	.71
31. Dialogue	.13	.09	-	.16	-.10	.65
Principal component solution:						
Eigenvalues	10.80	2.47	2.24	1.71	1.33	1.17
Proportion of variance	34.86	7.96	7.23	5.52	4.28	3.76
Varimax rotation solution:						
Eigenvalues	4.12	2.19	2.84	4.08	2.53	3.52
Proportion of variance	13.29	7.05	9.17	13.17	8.16	11.36

[1]The variables used to define each factor are listed in table C and are discussed on pages 12-16.

Table 9. Multiple regression analysis predicting criterion composites, age, sex, and race, using six TAT factor scores as predictors ($n = 1,910$)

Criterion variable	Multiple correlation	Highest single correlation	Proportion variance accounted for
1. Criterion factor I—school adjustment-----------------	.26	.22	.06
2. Criterion factor II—poor health--------------------	.04	.03	-
3. Criterion factor III—intellectual development-----	.59	.45	.34
4. Criterion factor IV—social adjustment-------------	.07	.05	-
5. Criterion factor V—emotional disturbance----------	.11	-.10	.01
6. Age--	.46	.38	.21
7. Sex--	.22	.14	.05
8. Race---	.39	.37	.15

Table 10. Means and standard deviations (SD) of six TAT composite scores, by age and sex ($n = 1,201$)

TAT factor and sex	6 years Mean	SD	7 years Mean	SD	8 years Mean	SD	9 years Mean	SD	10 years Mean	SD	11 years Mean	SD
Factor I—Verbal productivity												
Both sexes----	281.5	29.3	288.5	36.4	297.0	44.7	306.4	46.3	311.0	43.1	316.0	50.9
Boys------------	278.8	26.5	287.9	38.5	295.5	41.1	300.2	36.5	305.0	41.1	320.1	54.4
Girls------------	284.8	32.1	289.3	33.8	298.3	47.3	312.7	53.7	317.1	44.2	311.9	46.7
Factor II—Dysphoric mood												
Both sexes----	149.8	25.5	147.5	22.5	150.3	23.2	148.1	22.6	152.8	25.9	151.8	24.2
Boys------------	150.5	26.9	145.8	20.4	151.3	23.6	148.2	20.5	151.5	25.9	151.8	23.1
Girls------------	148.9	23.6	149.5	24.6	149.5	22.9	148.0	24.4	154.1	26.0	151.8	25.3
Factor III—Conceptual maturity												
Both sexes----	80.5	48.7	93.3	31.8	97.9	40.1	103.1	34.0	111.0	24.1	114.3	19.1
Boys------------	84.6	39.1	90.0	33.9	95.7	40.9	104.7	29.6	107.3	26.6	112.5	19.6
Girls------------	75.2	58.1	97.0	28.9	99.6	39.4	101.5	39.7	114.7	20.7	116.1	18.3
Factor IV—Narrative fluency												
Both sexes----	317.9	36.2	329.9	40.3	344.2	50.3	360.4	50.8	371.2	53.0	377.2	51.5
Boys------------	309.4	25.3	329.3	41.7	338.5	46.5	352.8	45.3	360.0	50.4	368.3	43.5
Girls------------	328.7	44.1	330.6	38.7	348.8	52.8	368.2	54.7	382.6	53.1	386.4	57.1
Factor V—Emotionality												
Both sexes----	294.0	31.3	295.1	30.0	300.1	35.0	300.2	33.0	304.7	41.2	306.2	42.5
Boys------------	295.0	31.5	294.9	27.8	299.7	36.7	301.4	36.5	303.3	43.4	307.2	34.4
Girls------------	294.0	31.1	295.3	32.3	300.3	33.6	299.0	29.0	306.1	38.8	305.1	49.5
Factor VI—Verbal fluency												
Both sexes----	228.8	25.7	237.1	27.5	250.4	51.1	253.9	41.0	263.3	49.7	266.6	52.8
Boys------------	224.8	17.8	237.4	29.7	246.3	45.3	250.2	38.9	254.1	41.4	263.1	45.9
Girls------------	233.7	32.3	236.8	24.6	253.7	55.2	257.7	42.3	272.6	55.2	270.3	58.9

APPENDIX I

DESCRIPTION OF THE SAMPLES

Cycle II of the Health Examination Survey

The samples of children for the two studies described in this report are subsets of the national probability sample of children aged 6-11 years examined during the second program (Cycle II) of the Health Examination Survey. The sample design for that survey was a multistage probability sample of persons in geographically defined segments of the U.S. population. Successive elements dealt with in the stages of selection of the sample are primary sampling units (PSU's), census enumeration districts, small clusters of households, individual households, and finally, the sample children. At the first stage, the nearly 2,000 PSU's into which the United States has been divided were grouped into 40 strata. One PSU was then selected from each of the 40 strata. Later stages of selection resulted in the selection of nearly 200 children aged 6-11 years from each of the 40 sample PSU's.

Examination of the sample children began in the first of the survey's 40 geographic locations (stands) in July 1963. The survey was completed in December 1965. Of the 7,417 children selected, the 7,119 who were examined—a response rate of 96 percent—gave evidence that they were a highly representative sample of children in the noninstitutionalized population of the United States (table I).

Study I Sample

To meet the primary objective of Study I (scale development) within requirements of budget and reliability, it was decided that the sample should consist of about 100 white boys and 100 white girls in each of the 6 single years of age in the 6-11 year age group for whom the Thematic Apperception Test (TAT) protocols were scorable and criterion data were complete. Since national representativeness was not an important factor in meeting the objectives of the pilot study, it was possible to begin the study as soon as data had been collected and processed for the required number of white children. The data for white sample children in 17 of the first 19 stands completed in Cycle II were reviewed for completeness and quality of TAT protocols. Sample children tested in the first two locations were eliminated from consideration because the TAT protocols for these two stands were manually recorded, whereas the TAT protocols were recorded on tape for all other stands. Of the 1,760 white children examined in Stands 3 through 19, 1,224 met the standards of completeness and quality of TAT protocol. Most of the elements of Study I were based on the sample of 1,224 children. However, for some elements of Study I it was additionally necessary to have complete criterion data for each child. From the 1,224 children in the Study I sample, 996 children were identified for whom complete

Table I. Health Examination Survey Cycle II sample, by sex, race, and age

Age	Both sexes				Boys				Girls			
	Total	White	Black	Other races	Total	White	Black	Other races	Total	White	Black	Other races
All ages--	7,119	6,100	987	32	3,632	3,153	464	15	3,487	2,947	523	17
6 years-------	1,111	950	156	5	575	489	84	2	536	461	72	3
7 years-------	1,241	1,063	172	6	632	551	79	2	609	512	93	4
8 years-------	1,231	1,035	192	4	618	537	79	2	613	498	113	2
9 years-------	1,184	1,019	158	7	603	525	74	4	581	494	84	3
10 years------	1,160	1,014	142	4	576	509	65	2	584	505	77	2
11 years------	1,192	1,019	167	6	628	542	83	3	564	477	84	3

Table II. Study I sample ($n = 996$) of white children, by sex and age

Age	Both sexes	Boys	Girls
All ages-----	996	505	491
6 years-------------	132	69	63
7 years------------	158	81	77
8 years-----------	183	94	89
9 years-----------	160	78	82
10 years-----------	188	94	94
11 years----------	175	89	86

criterion data were available. It is that smaller sample of 996 white children which was combined with another sample and used in some elements of Study II. The distribution of the Study I sample of 996 white children by age and sex is shown in table II.

Study II Samples

The research design of Study II consisted of four separate phases. To carry out these four phases, three samples of different size and composition were used in the Study II research: (1) from the total combined sample of 2,018 children, a reduced combined sample of 2,012; (2) a further reduced combined sample of 1,910 children; and (3) the national probability sample of 1,201 children selected to be representative of the larger HES national probability sample. The four phases and their corresponding sample sizes are:

● Development of criterion measures for validation of the TAT scales ($n = 2,012$)

● Development of measurement scales for the TAT using structural and thematic variables ($n = 1,910$)

● TAT scale validation ($n = 1,910$)

● Development of national norms ($n = 1,201$)

The national probability sample ($n = 1,201$) and the combined samples $n = 2,018$, $n = 2,012$, and $n = 1,910$ are described below.

National Probability Sample ($n = 1,201$).—The initial objectives of Study II—the development of TAT scales from a national sample of children and the estimation of norms on a national basis for the scales developed—required the study to be conducted on a nationwide probability sample of children. Due to budgeting limitations it was decided to conduct the study on only a subsample of the HES national probability sample of 7,119 children aged 6-11 years examined in Cycle II.

Specifications for selecting the subsample included the following points: the subsample should consist of approximately 1,200 children equally distributed by sex and single year of age (6-11 years) and approximately 200 of the 1,200 children should be black (Negro).

The subsample was selected by a random systematic sampling technique. A total of 1,268 children were selected from the children examined in Cycle II of the Health Examination Survey. Of this total, 211 were black children. The distribution of the probability subsample for Study II by age, sex, and race is shown in table III.

The national probability sample ($n = 1,201$) is the probability subsample from Cycle II of the Health Examination Survey described above reduced from 1,268 to 1,201 children as a result of the loss of 67 TAT protocols.

Specifically, 67 sample children were dropped because the TAT data were either inadequate or missing for the following reasons:

Table III. Total national probability sample ($n = 1,268$), by sex, race, and age (Study II)

Age	Both sexes			Boys			Girls		
	Total	White[1]	Black	Total	White[1]	Black	Total	White[1]	Black
All ages-------------	1,268	1,056	212	643	542	101	625	514	111
6 years-------------------	203	171	32	111	94	17	92	77	15
7 years-------------------	222	185	37	115	98	17	107	87	20
8 years-------------------	227	182	45	101	85	16	126	97	29
9 years-------------------	207	174	33	106	91	15	101	83	18
10 years------------------	203	175	28	104	87	17	99	88	11
11 years------------------	206	169	37	106	87	19	100	82	18

[1]Included with white children are one oriental 11-year-old boy and one oriental 6-year-old girl.

Table IV. The corrected stratified national probability sample ($n = 1,201$), by sex, race, and age (Study II)

Age	Both sexes			Boys			Girls		
	Total	White	Black	Total	White	Black	Total	White	Black
All ages ------------	1,201	1,006	195	610	515	95	591	491	100
6 years--------------------	188	162	26	105	89	16	83	73	10
7 years--------------------	207	173	34	111	94	17	96	79	17
8 years--------------------	218	176	42	97	83	14	121	93	28
9 years--------------------	200	168	32	101	87	14	99	81	18
10 years-------------------	191	166	25	96	81	15	95	85	10
11 years-------------------	197	161	36	100	81	19	97	80	17

Reason for loss	*Number of cases*
Inadequate testing time allowed	5
Examiner error	5
Atypical behavior of child (upset, refused to cooperate, etc.)	10
Retarded, deaf, blind, or special problems	7
Non-English speaking	4
Not recorded for other reasons (tape recorder not turned on, one or more cards omitted, etc.)	26
Tape recording technically inadequate for transcription	10

The distribution of the national probability sample of 1,201 children, the sample used in the final computation of normative information for the developed scales (phase four), by age, sex, and race, is shown in table IV. Although the age-sex-race composition of the probability subsample of 1,268 children (table III) seems not to have been seriously affected, the absence of the 67 TAT protocols cannot be completely ignored, particularly inasmuch as 10 cases were lost as a result of atypical behavior and seven for sensorimotor impairment or mental subnormality. However, the potential biasing effect of these omissions on the normative data is considered to be tolerable since they comprise such a small percentage of the total sample of 1,268 children.

Total Combined Sample (n = 2,018) and Reduced Combined Sample (n = 2,012). —For the developmental portion of Study II, the Study I sample and the national probability sample were combined to maximize the number of TAT protocol records on which the basic scales and statistical analyses were based so as to increase reliability of the data.

The total number in the combined sample is 2,018. That figure represents the sum of the 996 children of the Study I sample plus the 1,201 of the national probability sample with the exception of 179 children who were common to both samples. Furthermore, six children with incomplete criterion data were deleted in those phases of the study in which the criterion measures were developed and validated, reducing the sample to 2,012. The distribution of the total combined sample of 2,018 by age and sex is shown in table V. A note identifying age, sex, and color of the six deleted children is also included.

Further Reduced Combined Sample (n = 1,910). —In computing correlations among TAT variables and between TAT and criterion composites, phases two and three, a further reduction was necessary. This reduced combined sample consisted of 1,910 children after the exclusion of 49 children with manually recorded TAT protocols and 53 other children with incomplete data.

The TAT protocols for 49 children in the national probability sample selected from the first two stands of Cycle II had been manually recorded by the field examining psychologists. The 49 manually recorded protocols were compared with the tape-recorded protocols of Study I. An examination of the manually recorded protocols indicated two probable sources of bias which tended to reduce the length of stories for these children: (1) examiners asked questions which may have influenced the end of the story as defined in the scoring manual, and (2) at least one examiner did not record verbatim responses of the children; instead notations were made such as "describes room." A comparison of number of words per story between the Study I sample (mean = 88, SD = 70, n = 996) and the group of 49 manually recorded cases (mean = 54, SD = 38) indicated that the distributions differed significantly. In order to retain these 49 cases in the study, it would have been necessary to transform scores on

41

Table V. The combined Study I and II sample ($n = 2,018$), by sex, race, and age

Age	Both sexes			Boys			Girls		
	Total	White	Black	Total	White	Black	Total	White	Black
All ages--------------	2,018	1,823	195	1,035	939	96	983	884	99
6 years-------------------	303	275	28	172	[1]155	17	131	120	[1]11
7 years-------------------	340	305	35	176	[1]160	16	164	145	19
8 years-------------------	362	325	37	175	162	13	187	163	24
9 years-------------------	337	304	33	173	[1]158	15	164	146	18
10 years------------------	338	311	27	169	154	15	169	[1]157	[1]12
11 years------------------	338	303	35	170	150	20	168	153	15

[1]Sample was reduced to 2,012 children for development and validation of criterion measures by deletion of one child in each of these six categories.

"count" type items, such as number of words, to distributions with means and variances equivalent to those of the respective age-sex-race subgroups of children with tape-recorded stories. Unfortunately, other variables, such as dichotomous items, could not be adjusted by any rational scheme. It was finally decided to drop these 49 cases in the development and validation of the TAT scales.

Since the analysis of results in phases two and three involved correlational studies of composite scores, it was necessary to exclude 53 children in the national probability sample whose scores on one or more of the composite defining variables were lacking.

The distribution of the reduced combined sample of 1,910 children by age and sex is shown in table VI.

Table VI. TAT scale validation sample ($n = 1,910$), by sex and age

Age	Both sexes	Boys	Girls
All ages-----	1,910	990	920
6 years ------------	291	162	129
7 years ------------	324	175	149
8 years ------------	348	165	183
9 years ------------	314	160	154
10 years ------------	319	168	151
11 years ------------	314	160	154

———○○○———

APPENDIX II

TAT SCORING MANUALS

STRUCTURAL SCORING MANUAL

INTRODUCTION

Determining Story Length

Many of the items to be scored in accordance with this manual involve counting words, parts of speech, and other features of the story protocols in which accuracy and reliability of scoring are highly dependent on the precise identification of the story boundaries (beginning and end). The scorer should make this determination as the first step in the scoring of each story.

Instructions for Determining Story Boundaries

Beginning.—Ordinarily, the beginning of a story may be recognized by application of the following rules:

(a) Respondent (R) narrates a story or comments about the card after examiner (E) has asked him to "make up a story." The beginning of the story may be preceded by conversation between E and R.

(b) The *story* is not a specific reply to a specific question, such as "What do you see here?" followed by "I see a boy."

(c) If E asks R to tell a different story, score the first story only; disregard the second story.

(d) If R makes a spontaneous remark, such as "That boy is sad," and no further story is produced, either because of inability of R to elaborate or the intervention of questions by E, accept the remark as the story. In the event that no story at all is given, even if R answers specific questions by E, score the response as a rejection, item 1. In all cases of rejection of a card, no further scoring of that card for the particular R will be made under this manual.

Mark the story beginning on the protocol with a capital letter B or score rejection.

End.—Use the following rules to establish the end of a story:

(a) R indicates that the story is ended by a remark such as "That is all," "That is all I can think of,"

and the like. Such remarks establish the end of a story and are included as part of the story.

(b) R stops and E accepts the story as completed.

(c) E asks a question calling for interpretation which would thereby introduce content not spontaneously contributed by R, thus ending the spontaneous story. Questions such as "How does he feel?" and the like are in this category. Reflective statements by E do not constitute the end of the story.

(d) The following types of questions and comments by E encountered during a story are considered as *acceptable* questions or promptings and do not terminate a story:

(i) "Uh huh," "Go on," "Yes."

(ii) Repetition of a statement by R (frequently done when R's speech is inaudible or unclear, but also for encouragement).

(iii) "Tell me about it," "Tell me more." (Such statements reflect judgment by E in the examining situation and, while they may introduce extraneous variance in the story, are not arbitrarily condemned.)

(iv) The questions, "What happens then?" or "What is going on in your story?" are questionable, but are acceptable.

(v) E asks R to repeat a statement of his story. (Delete the portion of the repeated statement that paraphrases the original statement.)

Mark the story ending on the protocol with a capital letter E.

Inquiry.—The remainder of the protocol, following E, will be referred to as the "inquiry." Unless otherwise specifically stated in instructions for particular items, always score items in this manual only on the story content, defined by the boundaries B and E. Reference is made to other parts of the protocol for certain items, and in those cases the specific item instructions should be followed.

SCORING INSTRUCTIONS

1. CARD REJECTION. Score 1 for failure or refusal of R to produce a story in response to a card. Score 0 if not rejected. No further scoring is required if a card is scored 1 on this item.

(2.-4. IDENTIFICATION OF CHARACTERS.) The characters referred to in each story are classified in these items according to the following nomenclature. The first (two-digit) number in the double classification refers to *Type of character;* the second number refers to *Age status.* A character is defined as an animated being capable of communicating or feeling. Information in the inquiry may be used to establish role identity of characters.

Classifications should be written in three digits, combining the type of character (first two digits) and the age status (third digit) as stated in story or inferred by scorer from information given.

A. *Type of character*

(01) Self. Refers to narrator and applies only when story is in first person.

(02) Father. Refers to character in role of a father in the story.

(03) Mother. Refers to character in role of a mother in the story.

(04) Son. Refers to character in role of son in the story.

(05) Daughter. Refers to character in role of daughter in the story.

(06) Brother. Refers to character in role of a brother of another character in the story.

(07) Sister. Refers to character in role of a sister of another character in the story.

(08) Husband. Refers to character in role of husband.

(09) Wife. Refers to character in role of wife.

(10) Other male relative. Refers to character in role of grandfather, uncle, male cousin, or other male relative of another character in the story, including in-laws.

(11) Other female relative. Refers to character in role of grandmother, aunt, female cousin, or other female relative of another character in the story, including in-laws.

(12) Family. Collective reference to persons in the story as a family and not in any other way.

(13) Occupation. Refers specifically to persons such as teacher, doctor, burglar, policeman, or farmer having an occupational role in the story. The occupational title must be stated in the story. "A man plowing a field" would be scored as a man, not as a farmer; "a man operating" is scored as a man, but "a doctor operating" is scored as a doctor.

(14) Man. Adult male character, not a relative of another character.

(15) Woman. Adult female character, not a relative of another character.

(16) Boy. Young male character, not a relative of another character.

(17) Girl. Young female character, not a relative of another character.

(18) People. Collective reference to people, not otherwise specified.

(19) Animal. An animal as a character having a role in the story.

(20) Animals. Collective reference to animals as characters having roles in the story, not otherwise specified.

(21) Supernatural being. Refers to a ghost, spirit, elf, fairy, or other supernatural being as a character in the story.

(22) Supernatural beings. Collective reference to ghosts, spirits, elves, fairies, or other supernatural beings or characters in the story, not otherwise specified.

(23) Inanimate object(s). Includes dolls, manikins, robots, toys, etc., as characters having role(s) in the story.

(24) None.

(25) Character. Sex not identified, not related to other characters.

When there are conflicting roles, follow these rules:

(a) If a character has two roles, select the one related to the "main character" identified in items 2, 3, and 4. For instance, if the main character is a child, a woman who is both the child's mother and a wife would be scored as a mother.

(b) If the main character has multiple roles, select the role more closely related to the theme of the story.

If no character as defined by the character code is mentioned, score 240. An example of such scoring is as follows:

Card 1. "The ribbon unrolled." (240) The ribbon is not a character, capable of communication or feeling, as defined in this manual. If the story were to suggest that the ribbon acted in this way for some purpose, such as "to torment the boy's mother," then it would be a character, and the ribbon would be scored under category 23. In that case, the scoring would be 230.

B. *Age status*

Classify as accurately as possible from information given.

(0) Not applicable (used for character codes 12 and 19 through 25)

(1) Aged person

(2) Older adult, middle-aged person

(3) Younger adult, 20-30 year age range

(4) Youth, teenager, high school and junior high school age

(5) Boy or girl, 6-12 year age range

(6) Preschool child

(7) Infant

Character category (18) will be scored age 0 unless specified as children, then it will be (18), (4), (5), (6), or (7).

When age status of characters in the story is not specified or suggested, use the following guides:

Card 1: a boy (5)

Card 2: girl (4), woman (2), man (foreground) (2)

Card 5: woman (2)

Card 8 BM: man (with lantern) (2), man (with knife) (2), man (on table) (2), boy (foreground) (4)

If there is changing age status, score that age which corresponds to the dominant (i.e., principal) action of the story, or to the picture, if this is not sufficient. There may be multiple ages, corresponding to multiple dominant actions. If so, indicate only in character list. For example:

(04) (4) (3). This would represent a son who appears first as a youth and later as a young adult, with equally important actions at both age levels.

2. FIRST CHARACTER MENTIONED. Identify the first character mentioned in the story, using the three-digit code outlined above. The first reference to a character, although not completely identified, governs the scoring of this item. Thus reference by a pronoun (he, she, they) may establish precedence, even if identity is disclosed later, in the story or inquiry context. The following examples illustrate typical scoring decisions:

Card 5. "This lady's son was playing in the library." The score would be 032. The first character is *this lady*. Since the context identifies her as a

mother, she will be scored as (03) Mother. Since no specific information is given about her age status, follow the cues in the picture and score (2) Older adult.

Card 8 BM. "He has been shot in the stomach. We are trying to take it out. This boy is his grandchild." Score 102. The first character mentioned (He) is identified from the following context as the boy's grandfather. Score (10) Other male relative and (2) Older adult. Do not score age status as (1) Aged person, unless specifically indicated.

3. MOST DISCUSSED CHARACTER. Identify the character discussed most in the story, using the three-digit code outlined above. In most cases this should be an obvious decision. If it is necessary to compare the attention given to two or more characters, count the number of sentences in which each is mentioned. In the event of a tie, count the number of Main Character Modifiers, items 5-7, below, and score for the character having the largest number.

4. CENTRAL CHARACTER. Identify the central character and use the three-digit code outlined above. The central character is defined as the character to whom the point of the story is anchored and without whom the story would be incomplete. The following guidelines are suggested for identifying the central character.

(a) The central character is associated with the principal event in the story. For example, the figure popularly described as being operated on (card 8 BM) may appear to be the central character. However, in many stories, the person being operated on dies and the boy becomes grieved. The scorer must decide in such instances, whether the "patient" or the boy is to be scored as the central character, according to his judgment of the focus of the story.

(b) Other characters are usually identified in the story by their relation to the central character. For example, a teacher, mother, or father is frequently introduced in card 1 as "his teacher," "the boy's mother," or "the father of this boy."

(c) The character to whom affective reactions are attributed is usually the central character. For example, in card 1, "This little boy had been taking violin lessons and he feels sad because he doesn't want to take them anymore."

(d) The main character is usually involved in the outcome of the story. For example, in card 1, "He might be thinking that he is going to run away from home. He didn't."

In cases of extreme doubt in scoring item 4, score the character already most prominent in items 2 and 3.

If there is a group of characters defined separately, but as a group are the most discussed and are the central character, code as 180 but do not include on list of characters.

(5.-7. MAIN CHARACTER MODIFIERS.) The following instructions apply to the "main character" identified in items 2, 3, and 4. Follow them separately for each item. Count the number of words, including nouns, proper nouns, names, pronouns, and possessive adjectives in relation to the "main character" in the particular item.

5. MAIN CHARACTER MODIFIERS, ITEM 2. Count and record as instructed above.

6. MAIN CHARACTER MODIFIERS, ITEM 3. Count and record as instructed above.

7. MAIN CHARACTER MODIFIERS, ITEM 4. Count and record as instructed above.

8. LIST OF CHARACTERS. List all characters, in order of mention in the story, using the three-digit code outlined above. After each code number, write in on the scoring form any further characterization or detail mentioned in the story, such as name, age, role, etc., for each character.

9. OBJECTS MENTIONED. An object is something that can be manipulated—e.g., tool, toy, door, door knob, window (as in "She looked through the window"), modern conveniences, bullet. The central object is an object which is an integral part of the main action, and often indispensable. Multiple objects may be used as the central object. A face, music lessons, sky, and scenery are not objects. Score an object even though it is only mentioned as not being there (for example, "It is not a guitar, but a violin.").

List all objects mentioned in the story in the space designated on the scoring form. Animals referred to in the story which are not identified as characters should be recorded as objects. *First,* identify the central object, which is involved in the principal action of the story (for example, card 1, "is staring at his violin, wishing he were out playing baseball!"). Record this on the first line, designated *central object*. If no central object is mentioned, write *none*. *Second,* record all other objects, including animals not identified as characters, in the order mentioned in the story. When objects are referred to by pronouns (it, this) or indefinite nouns (something) and the identity is suggested by the context, write the suggested identity after the object word, in parenthesis. If no objects are mentioned, write *none* on the second line, designated *other objects*, as well as on the first line. Do not include place names, such as house, farm, field, etc., as objects.

10. PLACES MENTIONED. List all place words and names in the story in the space provided on the scoring form. Places are distinguished from objects by the

fact that they are loci of action and indicate where action takes place, but are not manipulated, as are objects. Examples of places are house, room, farm, field, roof, garage, garden, church, ranch, behind the door, under the bed, etc.

Indefinite references to a place are not scored, for example:

"There is a woman."

"Here is a man."

11. ACTION OR ACTIVITY. Write, in the space provided, a word, phrase, or sentence identifying the main action or activity in the story. For example, card 1, looking at the violin, wishing he were outside; card 2, plowing the field; card 5, looking in the room; card 8 BM, watching an operation, operating on a man, removing a bullet. The main action is usually associated with the central theme of the story and is most often performed by the central character. The following examples illustrate the recording of more than one main action.

Card 1. Boy wishes he were out playing; mother insists that he practice violin.

Card 5. Woman looks in bedroom; burglar goes out window.

12. REACTION TIME (RT) LATENCY (time latency between presentation of card and response). Record in seconds, as reported by E at end of story.

13. TOTAL TIME (length of story). Record in seconds, as reported by E at end of story.

14. NUMBER OF WORDS. Count number of words in story from point identified as *beginning* (B) to point identified as *end* (E). Do not count E's questions, interruptions, interpolated comments, or repetitions of words or phrases. Count auxiliary words separately (was playing is counted as two words), contractions as separate words (isn't is counted as though it were is not); titles or names are counted as words (Miss Mary Smith is counted as three words) and hyphenated words are counted as two words. Do not count statements reported by R in response to E's questions because of inability to understand.

15. POLYSYLLABIC WORDS. Count the number of different words (excluding variants) with three or more syllables that appear within the story, not including interpolated comments. Hyphenated words are not necessarily polysyllabic words, unless they have three or more syllables. Examples are the following:

operation, operated or operating (variants, scored once), instrument, wondering, remembering, somebody, everybody, violin

(16.-39. PARTS OF SPEECH.) Parts of speech are defined in this manual in accordance with J. N. Hook and E. G. Mathews, *Modern American Grammar and Usage.* New York: The Ronald Press Company, 1956. These definitions must be applied to the words as they appear in the story context. Count only words included in the word count in item 14. (References to the Hook and Mathews text are identified below by letters HM, followed by a page number.)

16. DESCRIPTIVE ADJECTIVES. Count the number of single or two-word (hyphenated) descriptive adjectives, which suggest physical or other characteristics of a noun, or express a judgment or opinion related to the noun. These include words of identification (e.g., mountain lion, Harvard student) and verbals (infinitives, gerunds, or participles) used as adjectives, which are always descriptive (e.g., living room, running water, dying soldier). Count hyphenated descriptive adjectives as one adjective. Do not include articles, demonstratives, possessives, relatives, interrogatives, indefinites, numbers, exclamatory words, or words of location. (HM 115)

17. COMPARATIVE ADJECTIVES. Count the number of comparative adjectives, whether used correctly or not. One-syllable adjectives normally form the comparative by the addition of -er or less (taller, less tall). Two-syllable adjectives are erratic in forming the comparative; those formed either by adding -er or employing more should be counted (e.g., happier, more happy, funnier, more funny, famouser, more famous).

18. SUPERLATIVE ADJECTIVES. Count the number of superlative adjectives, whether used correctly or not. These are formed by adding the suffix -est or by using most (e.g., most beautiful, prettiest, happiest, most funny).

19. POSSESSIVE ADJECTIVES. Count the number of possessive adjectives. Possessive adjectives are formed from nouns and pronouns which are adjectival in function and denote possession. Their primary purpose is to limit the application of the noun or pronoun (e.g., his mother, my book, boy's violin, father's gun). (HM 266)

20. ADVERBS. Count the number of one-word adverbs (not adverbial phrases) ending in -ly or their equivalents (e.g., beautifully, vigorously, thickly, justly, etc.). Equivalent adverbs include those which can have two forms, with or without the -ly (cheap, real, close, fair, late, loud, slow, thick, wrong), and those given by the child which may be grammatically incorrect. Adverbs often answer the question "How?". An adverb functions as a modifier of verbs, adjectives, adverbs, prepositional phrases, adjective clauses, or sentences. An example of each follows. (HM 289-293)

Modifier of verb: "The boy ran swiftly down the street." (Score only swiftly: do not score the adverbial phrase down the street.)

Modifier of adjective: "They lived in a real big house." (Real is considered to be an -ly equivalent.)

Modifier of adverb: "He ran very slow." (Score one one-word adverb, very modifies the adverb slow but is not scored.)

Modifier of phrase: "Early in the morning he went to school."

Modifier of clause: "The result is nearly what was expected."

Modifier of a sentence: "Obviously, the boy wanted to play the violin."

Do not score adverbs which do not take an -ly ending (down, far, how, long, much, never, not, once, out, since, soon, then, too, up, well, where, shy, fast, or very). (HM 295)

Do not score any of the following special functions of adverbs (HM 293) in this category: interrogative adverbs (how, when, why, where), exclamatory adverbs, transitional adverbs, relative adverbs, correlative adverbs, the expletive there, or independent adverbs (yes, no, and a few other words which stand alone as answers to questions).

A test for an adverb. Insert a form of be, seem, or become in place of the verb used. If these words make sense, the word used should be counted as an adjective; otherwise an adverb.

21. DIFFERENT ADVERBS. Count the number of different adverbs, as defined in item 20 in the story.

22. COMPARATIVE ADVERBS. Count the number of comparative adverbs, whether used correctly or not. A few adverbs cannot be compared, but most are compared by either adding -er or by employing more (quicker, faster, more slowly). Only adverbs defined in item 20 will be scored as comparative adverbs.

23. SUPERLATIVE ADVERBS. Count the number of superlative adverbs, whether used correctly or not. These are formed by adding the suffix -est or using most (e.g., quickest, most quickly, most slowly, fastest). Only adverbs defined in item 20 will be scored as superlative adverbs.

24. COMMON NOUNS. Count the number of common nouns. A common noun may refer either to something material or to an abstraction (e.g., class, path, man, star, pity, kindness, love). Include in this category other parts of speech such as gerunds used as nouns, but not pronouns. (Compare with items 25 and 26.)

25. PROPER NAMES. Count the number of different proper names given to characters, either animal or human. Count the whole name (given and surname, e.g., John Smith) as one name. Count only instances where a given or surname is used. Do not count titles (Mother, Father) used as specific reference.

26. OTHER PROPER NOUNS. Count all other proper nouns, referring to specific persons or places, not included in item 25. Proper nouns composed of more than one word (e.g., Christmas Eve) will be counted as a single proper noun. In the following examples, only (a), (c), and (e) are proper nouns, scored in this category. Include titles, names of days, months, organizations, holidays, seasons.

   (a) "Mother came into the room." (proper noun)

   (b) "Her mother came into the room." (common noun)

   (c) "If Winter comes, can Spring be far behind?" (proper noun)

   (d) "Nights are long in winter." (common noun)

   (e) "Where is the Sergeant?" (proper noun)

   (f) "One sergeant was killed." (common noun)

27. INDEFINITE NOUNS. Indefinite nouns can apply to people or to objects. In the former case they refer to people who have no role in the story, i.e., are not characters. For example, "People say he plays the violin well."

Indefinite objects are those which have no referent in the story, that is, they have no clear identity. For example, "Something wonderful happened."

Only the following are scored as indefinite nouns: people, folks, something, thing, nothing, when used as defined herein.

Count the number of indefinite nouns in the story. Indefinite nouns, such as folks, people, may be identified from the story context as having no clear referents. For example, folks, referring to folks in general, is indefinite, while folks, referring to my folks, has a referent.

28. PRONOUNS. Count only the following personal pronouns: I, you, he, she, we, they, me, him, her, us, them, himself, myself, except when used as a possessive pronoun or adjective (her book). (See items 19 and 30.)

29. USE OF THE FIRST PERSON. Count the number of first person singular pronouns (I, me, my, mine, myself) referring to the narrator or to a character in the story. "I" statements may appear either in interpolated comments or in the story. The following are examples of scorable personal references:

"I said, 'Give me that book.'" (two words)

"I told the story to my daddy how we were hunting." (two words, do not count we)

"This happened to me once." (one word)

"My mother is the same way." (one word)

"I don't know." (not as direct answer to E) (one word)

"That's all I can think of." (one word)

"I am playing the violin." (one word)

30. POSSESSIVE PRONOUNS. Count the number of possessive pronouns. The words, mine, yours, hers, his, theirs, and its, when used as pronouns, are defined as possessive pronouns (e.g., "His is the blue one." "The book is mine."). (HM 173) Score only the pronouns mentioned.

31. INDEFINITE PRONOUNS. Count the number of indefinite pronouns in the story. Indefinite pronouns, such as it, they, are pronouns used in a context in which the referent of the pronoun is indefinite. For example:

"They say it is wrong to do that."

"He played it."

In both cases, the underlined pronoun would be scored as indefinite only if the context fails to disclose a clear referent.

(32.-36. VERBS.) A verb is a word or group of words that expresses action, being, or state of being. Verbs are scored in this manual as: 32, single verbs; 33, complex verbs; 34, multiple verbs; 35, transitive verbs; and 36, intransitive verbs. Count each category as defined below. Items 32, 33, and 34 will overlap 35 and 36. If a verb is a multiple verb and one element of that multiple verb is complex, score both 33, complex verb, and 34, multiple verb.

Verbals (infinitives, participles, and gerunds) are scored as verbs when used as such. The participle is a verbal used as an adjective (see item 16). Gerunds are verbals used as nouns (see item 24). Generally, infinitives are scored as verbs depending on their function in the sentence. For example, in "To win is not easy," the phrase to win is used as a noun and the subject of the sentence. Therefore it is not scored as a verb, but as a noun. However, in "He likes to win," although used as a noun, the infinitive to win is the object of the verb likes and, the phrase "likes to win" is therefore counted as a complex verb.

32. SINGLE VERBS. Score as a single verb any verb, with or without auxiliary words, that is the only verb involved with a particular subject. Single verbs may have modifiers expressing tense or mood, such as is eating, is going to play, was supposed to play, had been studying, is about to leave, didn't like.

Sometimes the word going is used as part of a single verb, as in the second example above to express developing (future) action. However, this usage must be distinguished from that in which going is a verb in its own right, as in "going to school." In the latter sense, going may also be coupled with an infinitive ("going to school to play") and would then be a complex verb, item 33.

Other examples of single verbs are:

"He wants him to win." The subject he involves only the verb wants; him is the subject of the infinitive to win. This sentence is therefore scored as including two single verbs.

"The boy ran and the girl walked." Score as two single verbs.

"There's somebody playing a violin." The word there is classed as an expletive and has no function except to start the sentence. The subject somebody involves the contracted verb is and the predicate nominative playing. Score as a single verb.

Additional single verbs are:

"She keeps harping at him to play the violin." (two single verbs)

"He ended up being one." (one single verb)

"He grew up to be Jack Benny." (one single verb)

33. COMPLEX VERBS.
Score verbs coupled with infinitives ("He wants to play") and verbs coupled with verbal phrases ("He is thinking about playing") as complex verbs. Disregard the number of couplings. Thus, "He wants to go to play," and "He wants to go," would both be scored as complex verbs.

34. MULTIPLE VERBS.
Score two or more verbs related in a sentence to a subject as multiple verbs, as in the following example:

"He went to his music lesson, played the violin for his teacher, and rode the bus home." The subject he takes the verbs went, played, and rode.

35. TRANSITIVE VERBS.
Score as transitive all verbs that express "someone doing something to somebody or something." Transitive verbs must have an actor and a receiver of the action. They may also be in either active or passive voice, as in the following examples:

"The boy played the violin." (active voice)

"The violin was played by the boy." (passive voice)

In the following sentence the first verb is transitive, while the second is intransitive:

"The girl took a pill and felt better."

This sentence should also be scored as a multiple verb (item 34).

36. INTRANSITIVE VERBS.
Score all remaining verbs as intransitive verbs. The distinguishing feature of intransitivity is the absence of a receiver of the action. An intransitive verb can have no passive voice form (HM 224). Examples of intransitive verbs are:

"The boy plays well."

"Children are playing."

The following linking verbs are usually intransitive except when used as auxiliary verbs (included in single verbs in this manual): am, is, was, were, seem, become, appear, prove, look, remain, feel, taste, smell, sound, turn, and grow.

(37.-38. SIMPLE EXCLAMATIONS.)
Count the number of simple exclamations by R (Wow!, Gee!, Whee!, Hot diggety!, Oh!, Oh, thank goodness!). The word well is frequently used to fill pauses and is not scored as an exclamation. Exclamations which precede the story proper and occur while R and E are discussing the task should be scored here. Do not count simple exclamations accompanied by comments such as "My goodness, that man is being operated on," "Oh boy, this is a hard one." These are scored under item 38.

38. EXCLAMATIONS ACCOMPANIED BY COMMENTS.
Exclamations such as the last two examples in item 37, whether in or preceding the story, should be scored in this category. Count the number of such exclamations given.

39. EXPLETIVES.
Expletives are words having only the function of introducing a sentence or statement. They are used as a sign, without special meaning. For the purpose of this manual, count there, here, now, it (usually followed by "is," an indefinite), well, as expletives. Record the number of expletives in the story.

40. QUESTIONS.
Record the number of direct or indirect questions asked by any story character. A direct question is in dialogue while an indirect question is in narrative. For examples, "The boy said, 'Can you play the violin?'" is a direct question, but "The boy asked the girl if she could play the violin," is an indirect question.

(41.-45. INTERPOLATIONS.)
These items refer to interpolated remarks, which may be asides or digressions from the continuity of the story narrative made by R. Interpolations need not be complete sentences. They should be scored only within the story proper (between points identified as beginning and end of story) and only when made spontaneously by R. Remarks made in response to questions or comments by E are not to be counted as interpolations.

41. NUMBER OF INTERPOLATIONS. Count the number of separate interpolated statements (not the number of words). One word interpolations, such as "Gee!" may also be scored an exclamation, item 37. Examples of interpolations are given under item 42.

42. NUMBER OF INTERPOLATION WORDS. Count the total number of words in the interpolated statement identified for item 41. The following are examples of scorable interpolations:

> "That's all, I guess." (five words; that's is scored as two words)

> "The boy was walking along, you know, and he . . . ." (two words)

> "I can't think of anything else." (six words; can't is equivalent to cannot, one word)

43. INTERPOLATIONS REFERRING TO R. Count the number of interpolations involving self-references by R in which he relates himself to the story content, or to a story character. For example, on card 1, R may say, "He feels the same as I do about practicing the violin." Do not include interruptions, as defined in item 45.

44. INTERPOLATIONS REFERRING TO E. Count the number of interpolations in which R makes a reference to E, such as, "He looks like you." Such comments as "you see, you know" or simply, "See . . . ." are not scored here but are scored under items 41 and 42.

45. INTERRUPTIONS. Count the number of interpolations which represent interruptions of the testing situation by R, such as, "I have to go to the bathroom."

46. PAUSES. A pause is indicated by the typist by a dash, statement, or periods (e.g., "um," PAUSE---). Count pauses only within the story boundaries.

47. VERBATIM REPETITIONS. Count all occurrences within the story of immediate reuse of the same word or group of words. Do not count repetitions within interpolated comments. Examples of repetitions are the following:

> "He took his horse out there with a—with a plow." (one repetition)

> "Once there was a—Once there was a man who lived in a—lived in a house." (two repetitions)

48. CORRECTIONS. Count the number of instances in which corrections occur in the story, not including interpolated comments. Corrections may be regarded as a form of self-monitoring of speech. Whenever R corrects or changes a statement to make it clearer, more exact, or to alter the meaning, count the change as

a correction. Do not count repetitions as corrections. The following are examples of corrections that should be scored:

> "It was a — to him it was a — ."

> "She had a cat, I mean a dog."

> "The woman was going to move into the house. Well, no. She didn't want to move in the house."

(49.-50. DIALOGUE.) Score dialogue when the form of narration involves statements by characters that should be placed in quotations. Dialogue may involve occasional quotable statements (item 49) or conversations between two or more characters (item 50). In some cases, the second character may be inferred and does not participate in the conversation. Such instances should usually be scored under item 49.

49. DIALOGUE, QUOTES. Score this item for any statements that should be in quotations for any character in the story, but do not count two-way conversations for this item. A whole story in the first person should be scored. Also score instances such as "The sign read 'Wanted—Someone to do cleaning.'"

50. DIALOGUE, CONVERSATION. Score as present if conversations occur between two or more characters.

51. SPEECH IMPAIRMENT. The responsibility for detecting speech impairment of R has been assigned to the transcription reviewer (auditor). Such defects are noted by the typist and include: STAMMER, STUTTER, CLEFT PALATE. Score if any such indication appears on the transcript. If an excessive number of "uh's" or the like appear in the transcript, the tape should be checked for speech impairment even if not noted by the auditor.

52. SPEECH INCOHERENCE OR UNINTELLIGIBILITY. Detection of incoherence or unintelligibility of the narrated story has also been assigned to the transcription reviewer (auditor). The word MUMBLES is used to indicate speech incoherence. Score if this appears on the transcript.

53. SITUATION COMPLEXITY. The complexity of the situation developed in the story should be scored according to the following classification:

(1) *No situation.* Use this category when there is no discernible action situation. This occurs when R enumerates persons or objects in the picture (boy, horse, tree) or describes a scene (in present or historical perspective *without any action,* "That is a farm scene," "This is a man," "These people just came from Boston . . . .").

(2) *Simple action situation.* For the purpose of this manual, a simple action situation involves a single action in progress. Dramatically, it is a simple scene in a play. The action, occurrence, or event transpires as the scene unfolds and does not involve reference to antecedent or consequent events or explanation of a plot beyond the action taking place.

(3) *Complex action situation.* A situation is considered complex if the scene of action shifts during the story in time or place, or if the plot involves activity of greater complexity than the limited action situation described in (2).

54. CONTRADICTION. Contradiction is scored if the story contains statements of mutually incompatible ideas. If a contradiction is found which R has corrected, whether in the same sentence or later in the story, do not score it as a contradiction (it should be scored as a correction). Contradictions therefore appear to be made without awareness on the part of R. Contradictions between meanings expressed about the same persons, objects, or events in different parts of the story should be noted and scored. Several types of contradiction are illustrated in the following examples.

"People for miles would walk to buy books because their children didn't have any books to listen to." (contradictory sense words)

"One day there was this man and she wanted to buy a store." (contradictory sex role)

"She said, 'Do you want to go to the store?' and he said 'yes.' So we went to the store." (projects self as story character previously identified as not-self)

"They told her to work, and then they said that he could quit." (contradictory sex role)

"They were playing on the baseball diamond and he made a touchdown."

55. QUEER VERBALIZATIONS. Note any unusual or deviant expressions, whether considered pathological or not. The following examples illustrate types of expressions that should be noted under this item. Record all expressions noted in the space provided on the record sheet.

"...his father will give it for him on the whole rest of the life."

". . . up in the sky God thinks like they ain't going to ruin theirs because there's going to be a thunder storm. . . ."

"They need all the equipment they can do to get the bullet out."

"And there were branches of trees and bunches of felled down trees and a forest fire."

"They order a hole, but there wasn't very much water there."

"They turned upside down some lamps and some panicking."

"This is church time ... there was plows of rows to everybody that's staying."

"He asked his mother if he could go to violin music and learn how ...."

56. MISPERCEPTIONS. Note all instances in which R misidentifies elements of the picture. Include in this category age misrepresentations to an extreme degree. This item is not scored on card 16. The following are some examples:

Card 1. boy referred to as a man; violin referred to as a beartrap, machine gun, train, etc. (violin referred to as fiddle, guitar, or banjo is acceptable)

Card 5. figure of woman identified as a man or boy

Card 8 BM. identification of the figure in the foreground as a woman or girl

57. STORY (OR PICTURE) TITLE. Score if R gives the story a title. List title on scoring sheet.

(58.-62. COMPLIANCE WITH INSTRUCTIONS.) Items 58 through 62 are designed to measure compliance with the examiner's instructions.

58. PAST REFERENCE. Credit any reference to things, events, or situations which have taken place in the past and may be considered as antecedent to the present action of the story. The reference may be to either the immediate or remote past, but should be acceptable as antecedent to the present action.

59. PRESENT REFERENCE. Credit if the story includes any activity or behavior that is in the process of occurring within the story. For example:

"He's thinking about his violin that he got for his birthday."

"He wants to become a violinist."

60. FUTURE REFERENCE. Future reference is credited if any reference is made to things, events, or situations which take place in the future, i.e., after the time of the scene pictured on the card as described in the story. References may be to immediate or remote future but must be to definite things, events, or situations. In some instances, outcome, item 63, and this item will both be scored alike for the same material. However, a future event may occur when there

is no outcome to the story and vice versa. For example:

> "His mother wants him to play the violin. He hates it so much that <u>one day he will break all the string on his violin and throw it out the window</u>."

> "<u>He will grow up to be a violinist</u>."

61. EXPRESSION OF FEELING. Any indication of an expression of feeling or emotion on the part of any of the characters in the story is credited. "Wishing" and "wanting" may be considered as "feeling" for the scoring of this item. For example:

> "...he doesn't know how to play it and he's <u>sad</u>."

> "He <u>wants to learn</u> to play it."

62. REFERENCE TO "THINKING." Credit any expression of thinking, recalling, or related cognitive behavior such as deciding, believing, realizing, wondering, and the like. For example:

> "He is thinking about becoming a famous musician."

63. OUTCOME. Credit any reference to an ending or outcome to the events or situations which take place in the story, whether or not as a consequence of the activity or behavior that is in the process of occurring.

64. TONE OF OUTCOME. This item will be scored zero (0) if no outcome is given. If an outcome is given, score (1) *happy*, (2) *unhappy*, or (3) *neutral*.

(1) Score $\underline{1}$ for *happy ending* or optimistic outcome. For example:

> Card 8 BM: "The boxer was hurt and had to stay in the hospital. Then this thing healed up and he got to box again....He won the fight. He won the second fight. And then he was champ again."

> Card 1: "...the boy learned how to play the violin when he grew up to become a great musician."

(2) Score $\underline{2}$ for *unhappy ending* or pessimistic outcome. For example:

> Card 1: "...he broke all the strings on his violin and threw it out the window."

> Card 8 BM: "...it was something in his stomach and they had to operate and cut it open. The boy was worried. Finally, his father died."

(3) Score $\underline{3}$ for *neutral ending* or outcome. For example:

> Card 1: "Then she just found it, and she wondered who owned it."

Card 2: "He's plowing a garden. He will spend much time thinking whether he should make it bigger or just leave it like it was."

65. LEVEL OF INTERPRETATION. Classify each story as to level of interpretation according to the following criteria:

(1) *Enumeration.* Score $\underline{1}$ if R enumerates the stimuli on the card (boy, table, thing).

(2) *Description.* Score $\underline{2}$ if R describes the scene on the card but provides no interpretations as defined below.

> "There is a young boy sitting at a table with a violin. The boy is sad."

(3) *Interpretation.* Score $\underline{3}$ if R interprets the character's feelings, behavior, etc., in terms of a causal or purposeful relationship. However, the causal or purposeful relationship may be implied and is not necessarily scored as items 66 or 67.

> "He feels sad because his mother died."

> "He wants to learn to play so he can become a great musician."

66. CAUSALLY CONNECTED STATEMENTS. This item is intended as an elaboration of item 65, Level of Interpretation. Causally connected statements involve a related action (feeling, behavior, etc.) which occurs in the same or adjacent sentences. The reason for such action should be given or inferred, and the consequence of the action should be expressed. For example:

> "Her father brought home a birthday cake. That is why the mother wanted her to come home."

> "The woman promised to pay him fifty cents an hour because he needed the money so bad."

> "The horse broke his leg so the man shot him."

> "He feels sad because his mother died."

67. PURPOSEFULLY CONNECTED STATEMENTS. This item is also intended as an elaboration of item 65, Level of Interpretation. Purposefully connected statements involve a related action (feeling, behavior, etc.) which occurs in the same or adjacent sentences. The reason for such action should be given or inferred; the consequence of the action is on the actor, and a goal-oriented activity is implied or occurs. Some examples follow:

> "This lady was getting ready for bed. She heard a noise in the next room. So she looked out the door to see what it was."

> "The boy was hungry so he ate an apple."

THEMATIC SCORING MANUAL

INTRODUCTION

The rules for determining story boundaries and the definitions of terms given in the Structural Scoring Manual also apply to this manual. Following is a set of procedures for scoring the TAT for thematic content.

SCORING INSTRUCTIONS

Enter the sample number, age, and sex of respondent (R) on the Thematic Scoring Sheet in the spaces provided.

1. CARD REJECTION. Code each card 1 (rejected) or 0 (not rejected) in accordance with the instructions in the Structural Scoring Manual. No further thematic scoring is required if a card is scored 1 on this item.

2. THEMATIC RESPONSE. A theme is defined as part or whole of the story proper which involves some expressed interaction between one or more characters (persons or animals) and an environmental press. Use definition of characters as in the Structural Scoring Manual. As in that manual, animated objects (e.g., a dancing doll) may be treated as characters. Three levels of thematic response are distinguished as follows:

Score 0—*No theme.* For example:

Card 1: B [Beginning]. "There's a boy." E [End].

Card 2: B. "It's a house. It's a lady with Bibles. It's a other lady. It's a man..It's a horse. It's a wheats or something, and it's some rocks." E. (Lacks minimal interaction between character and environmental press.)

Card 5: B. "There are some flowers with a lamp. The lamp's over there. There's a table. There's a door." E.

Score 1—*Thematic content* (not elaborated). A story in which the essential elements of interaction of a character and an environmental press are present but not developed into a coherent story. Themes which lack one or more of the criteria which define thematic elaboration in 2, below, are scored here. For example:

Card 1: B. "He has his hands in his ears. He's looking at an instrument. There's a piece of paper like on bottom." E. (Satisfied criterion minimal interaction between character and environmental press.)

Card 1: B. "The boy feels sad. It looks like he's getting ready to play his gui...violin. It looks like he's worried about something too." E.

Card 2: B. "Lady's walking home, I guess from school—Like they're planting vegetables. Lady's going in the house—and she sees some barns back there. There's a lady lay—up—leaning—up against a tree. Looks like—the lady with the books looks like she's walking to school." E. (This is an example of an item which borders on the "no theme" response, but the minimal criterion was judged to be satisfied by the underlined elements.)

Card 2: B. "It looks like a man is planting food. It looks like that girl's going to school, or she's worried about something. The man and the lady are looking at something." E.

Card 5: B. "It looks like the lady's surprised." E. (Environmental press is implied.)

Score 2—*Thematic elaboration.* A response in which a theme is presented in a coherent story. This "coherent story" should contain:

(a) One or more indications of "feeling" or "thinking" by a character

(b) Goal behavior

(c) An outcome

A coherent story is defined as one which has the essential elements integrated and organized. The story should be something more than a series of relatively unrelated statements, and there should be an apparent effort to present a story which has a plot. This definition excludes stories which are primarily descriptive of the situation or action.

3. REPRESENTATION OF MANIFEST CONTENT OF CARD. The question here concerns whether or not R included in the story the persons, animals, objects, and locales depicted in cards 1, 2, 5, and 8 BM. For each card, score each item listed on the scoring sheet as 1 (present) or 0 (absent). The underlined items below are arbitrarily designated as major.

The card content items listed below are intended to provide a means of anchoring objects and characters in the story to the stimuli on the card. Synonyms or generic terms should be scored as manifest content of the related items. The objects scored must be specified in the story, but if mentioned, the objects are scored regardless of their significance to the story. Misidentification or misperceptions are not scored on this item but are scored on item 4.

Card 1. boy, violin, bow, table, chair, sheet music

Card 2. girl, young woman; older woman, mother; man, adult male person (in foreground); books; farm scene, country scene; horse, white horse; horse, black (dark) horse (in background); furrows, plowed field, row; barn(s), house(s); lake, river, water; hill(s); sky; tree(s) (NOTE: rocks are not scored)

Card 5. woman, middle-aged woman; half-opened door, doorway; room; lamp, light; table; flowers, vase, flowers in vase; sideboard (or equivalent); bookends, books; bookcase (on wall)

Card 8 BM. boy, youth; man, father (on operating table); man, doctor (with knife); knife; rifle, gun, barrel of rifle; operation scene (reverie); other man

Scoring rules:

The object listed must be specified in the story. A synonym or generic term is accepted as equivalent to the object listed.

Content representation is scored as follows, if not otherwise specified:

Card 1: Any mention of a single character (he, him, person, etc.) is scored as boy. The following are acceptable names for the violin: fiddle, viola, instrument.

Card 2: If only a single character is included in the story, score as girl unless otherwise specified. An indefinite reference to a group of characters (i.e., family) will be scored as girl, woman, man (foreground), unless otherwise indicated by the story content. If, in addition to the girl (lady, person with books), another indefinite character is given, score older woman. If, in addition to the girl, a plural pronoun is used to describe characters, score older woman and man, unless otherwise specified.

Card 5: Mention of a single character is scored as woman.

Card 8 BM: Mention of a single character is scored as boy unless specified in the story. Indefinite reference to characters (they) will be scored as doctor and other man, e.g., "They're cutting on him" would be scored as father, doctor, and other man. In cases where the operation scene is "imagined" or dream content and the boy is thinking of himself as being on the operating table, score both boy and father.

4. MISPERCEPTION. Score each of the card content items listed above in item 3 for cards 1, 2, 5, 8 BM for accuracy of perception of objects and characters presented. Score each item 0 if identified accurately and 1 if incorrectly identified. Incorrect identification is defined as gross error in age (man for boy), sex, species (cow for horse), role (father for boy), or other significant attribute.

Scoring rules: Misidentification is sufficient to score this item.

Card 1: "picture," score sheet music; "belt," score bow; "it," "whatcha-ma call it," "bear trap," "tank," "guitar," "piano," score violin

Card 2: "guy," score girl (provided reference is to the central character in the story)

Card 5: "he," score woman

Card 8 BM: "woman" or "mother" on the operating table, score father; "woman" or "mother" in the role of the "doctor," score doctor

5. CHARACTER REFERENCE INCOHERENCE. Incoherence of character reference is defined as disagreement between nouns or pronouns of reference and the antecedents to which they refer. Grammatical errors of tense or number are not included. If no incoherence is found in the story, score 0; indicate a number (1 or higher) to record the number of instances of incoherence in the story.

The incoherent reference must be to a character:

Card 1: "The boy in this picture is looking at a violin. She — he wonders whether he will play it."

Card 5: "He was thinking where she could be so he—she— he went back home."

Card 5: "So I went back to sleep ....when she got up her face was all different."

The following example is *not* scored here (but should be scored under item 4 as a misidentification).

"I was supposed to be practicing piano before I ate. So I finally practiced violin and then I ate my lunch."

6. MORBID MOOD QUALITY. A story theme is considered morbid if it expresses ideas of a depressed, extremely gloomy, gruesome nature, or preoccupation with disease, or death. Statements involving cutting out someone's heart, internal organs falling out, and gruesome accidental death or murder are examples of morbid quality. Score morbid quality present 1; not present 0.

A theme may be bizarre but not morbid, morbid but not bizarre, both, or neither.

These two examples should be scored as morbid mood quality:

Card 5: "The girl fell all the way down and she was dead. The mother cried, and the father cried. They buried her. Then there wasn't any girl for her mother, and her mother was sad and started bawling all night and all day."

Card 16: "The car smashed him. He didn't wake up the next morning. He's dead. He didn't have enough time to disintegrate. When he disintegrated, he looked awful bad. He didn't like to pass on, but he did."

Preoccupation with death refers to death abstractly or to one's own death. Preoccupation with killing someone else is not scored here, but is scored under item 20e, if threatening to kill, and 20h and i if death occurs through violence.

7. BIZARRE THEME. A theme may be morbid, but not bizarre, bizarre but not morbid, both, or neither. Bizarre themes lack orientation to reality, suggest distorted, nonlogical thought processes, or represent socially deviant behavior (e.g., cannibalism) to an extreme degree. Crimes of murder or robbery are not bizarre in and of themselves, nor are humanlike behavior of animals (e.g., Mickey Mouse) or "fairy tale" content. Science fiction content (e.g., man from outer space) in and of itself is not scored as bizarre. Score bizarre thematic content 1, and absence of bizarre content 0.

The following excerpts from stories are given to illustrate scoring of this item:

Card 5: "Well, her face was real pretty. Then when she looked out it turned to bricks. Turned into bricks. She couldn't move her eyes or mouth."

Card 8 BM: "He's cutting him up to eat him—to eat him for dinner."

Card 16: "They would cut him up and eat him and then would save the rest for the other eating dinner."

Card 16: "The alligators will climb up in your hair and you'll have alligator hair forever."

8. RELIGIOUS EMPHASIS. Religious emphasis is reflected in the following themes: (a) those devoted to religious topics, (b) those in which significant story characters have roles as priests or ministers, or have Biblical names such as Baby Jesus, Joseph, Mary, or God, or (c) those in which the Bible, Noah's Ark, or other references to religion are essential aspects. If religious emphasis is present, score 1; if not, score 0.

Excerpts from stories which illustrate the scoring of this item follow:

Card 2: "A girl's going to church."

Card 2: "...the missionary's bringing all this food to them."

Card 2: "She was trustful for God and she always liked God ...."

Card 8 BM: "They thought God was a piece of junk."

Card 16: "Well, this is a picture of God, and he is up in heaven."

9. CONFUSION OF R. Score 1 if R makes a remark indicating that he feels confused, such as, "I'm all mixed-up," "I'm crazy," or "I'm confused." If confusion is absent, record 0.

10. ESCAPE. Escape is defined as any action in a story in which any character expresses thought or action which has the effect of avoiding persons or situations by running away or otherwise escaping, including going to sleep. Only *overt* acts of escaping or attempting to escape are scored. Score positive instances of escape 1, absence of escape 0.

Scoring rule: The idea of escaping must be implicit in the story; the fact that an unpleasant or aversive situation exists is not justification for scoring this item.

Illustrations of story excerpts properly scored here:

Card 2: "Then she's going to go and run away."

Card 8 BM: "At the ending, he escaped from the enemies and he went home safely."

Card 8 BM: "Tom started to watch but then he couldn't stand it any longer." (This represents a borderline case which may be scored here.)

Card 16: "The fox beat him to his hole and chased the rabbit into the forest." (NOTE: the rabbit escaped.)

11. EGOCENTRISM. Egocentrism is considered present if the theme is focused on the feelings, thoughts, or actions of a single character without evidence of any awareness of the reactions or feelings of other persons. Score presence of egocentrism 1, absence 0.

Illustrations of story content properly scored here follow:

Card 1: The theme is concerned only with the boy and his feelings or actions.

Card 2: The girl with the books is usually the focal character. This card is scored here if the other characters are ignored or handled at a very superficial level of description and the focal character is given dynamic attributes (not merely described).

Card 5: The theme is concerned only with the woman and her feelings or actions. A burglar may appear as a threat to the focal character but is treated as an object of fear rather than a person.

Card 8 BM: The boy in the foreground is dreaming or fantasizing and the story is focused on his thoughts or dreams; or the story is focused on the boy to the exclusion of the operation scene characters.

12. FANTASY. Fantasy is considered involved if the theme is set totally or partly in a framework of dreams or daydreams, or if any character expresses dreams or daydreams in the story. Score presence of fantasy 1, absence of fantasy 0.

The inference concerning dreaming or daydreaming must be explicit in the story. Indications of reverie in thought are not scored here ("thinking" was scored as item 62, Structural Manual).

Examples properly scorable here:

Card 8 BM: "In his sleep he was dreaming this."

Card 8 BM: "He's dreaming that these two men are getting ready to cut him open."

Examples of reverie *not* scorable here:

Card 8 BM: "He was thinking about that he had to go to hospital and they were going to cut him open."

Card 2: "She's thinking what she would do when she grows up."

13. FEAR. Look for any expression of fear, dread, or phobia; mild states of worry or anxiety are excluded from this definition. Indications of fear include reactions to threat involving screaming, being scared, shaking with fear, or being terrorized. Phobic indications include overt or implied fears or excessive concern with specific objects, such as snakes, alligators, rats, ghosts, the dark, storms, etc. Score presence of fear 1, absence of fear 0.

Excerpts of stories which are properly scored here follow:

"It was chillers from science fiction and she was scared."

"He starts wiggling around and screaming."

"The dog started barking at her. She was almost ready to scream. She went out of the house, shaking."

14. WEALTH POSSESSED OR ACQUIRED. This category focuses on themes involving wealth or riches, indicated by the possession or acquisition of wealth, including symbols of wealth such as valuable (not costume) jewelry, mink coat, inheritance, riches, etc. Score mention of wealth possessed or acquired 1, absence 0.

Illustrations of story excerpts properly scored here follow:

Card 5: "The man received a big reward for capturing a bandit."

Card 8 BM: "...Then he became a famous doctor, and he got a lot of money and was very wealthy."

NOTE: The mere saving of money through one's labor or stealing money should not be scored here. The intent is to score the subject's values concerning wealth, not his industriousness or honesty. If he saved a million dollars, that should be scored here.

15. WEALTH LOST. Score 1 for any mention of the loss of wealth, including theft of valuables or changing status from rich to poor; absence of wealth lost is scored 0.

The loss must be extreme. The burning down of one's house would not be scored unless the context indicated the house was a very valuable one.

The temporary loss of an item of wealth is *not* scored, i.e., "The maid stole a sum of money from a man but the police caught her."

The value of the item should be substantial. The following would *not* be scored here:

"Her favorite vase and some money on the table were stolen."

16. POVERTY. Score 1 for any mention of poverty or serious economic deprivation, such as being poor, not having enough food or clothing, or having to beg. If poverty is not mentioned or suggested, score 0.

The following illustrations are properly scored here:

Card 2: "This family with very many children—they lived in the city and found out it was much too expensive for them to live."

Card 8 BM: "...in the past, he and his father, they were very poor and the father needed an operation."

17. PROJECTION. Score 1 if R, either directly or by an apparent slip of the tongue, includes himself (or herself) in the story. Do not score as projection first-person dialogue quotations ("I'm going to play," said Pete). If projection is absent, score 0.

The following are illustrations of items properly scored here:

Card 1: "Once upon a time my little boy was playing a violin."

Card 5: "Once upon a time a burglar came in my house, and I was sleeping."

Card 16: "When I got home I was happy that I had a fun time at the beach."

18. HOSTILE ANTAGONISM. Antagonism is defined as intense conflict or negative affective relations between story characters. Instances of resentment, rejection, willful disobedience, expressions of an adverse emotional relationship, unprovoked aggressive acts, and intense rivalry for the affections of another person

are included in this definition. Each of the four interpersonal patterns listed below should be scored separately. Score 1 for the presence of hostile antagonism, and 0 for the absence.

There should be no doubt in the scorer's mind that the interpersonal relationship is antagonistic. Disagreement with respect to what one likes or dislikes or difference of opinion is not sufficient indication of antagonism to score here. The element of hostility should be present in order to score items (a) through (d).

If antagonism is evidenced between the child and the parents, score both (a) and (b) for this item.

(a) *Mother-child*

Card 5: "There were these little children and her mother—their grandmother—this their mother couldn't put up with them."

Card 5: "And afterwards I didn't feel so good because she hit me."

(b) *Father-child*

Card 2: "She was mad because her father was just standing there working and paying no attention to her."
Card 16: "His father had heard that he went so his father went up there and got him and brought him home. One night his father killed him."

(c) *Mother-father*

Card 8 BM: "So one time his father got married. One time the wife didn't like him—her husband. She didn't like him so that she cut him."

(d) *Child-sibling*

Card 5: "So their mother came in and they started fighting."

19. AFFECTION. The interpersonal relationship must be spelled out in the story to be definitely one of loving affection. Affection is defined as a positive, pleasant, emotional relationship between story characters. Instances of justifiable discipline do not preclude scoring this item. Each of the same four patterns listed above in item 18 should be scored separately. Score 1 for the presence of affection, and 0 for absence.

If affection is evidenced between the child and the parents, score both (a) and (b) for this item.

20. ATTRIBUTES OF CHARACTERS. Each card is to be scored separately for the presence or absence of each of the traits, states, or conditions of characters, as defined below. Score 1 if the characteristic is present; otherwise score 0.

The traits or characteristics specified in (a) through (d) must be attributable to a character and must be spelled out. The manifestation of behavior

which merely suggests that the person may possess such traits is not sufficient evidence to score these items.

(a) *Kind, loving, rewarding.* A character helps, teaches, loves, rewards, shows kindness, or other positive affect toward another character. For example:

Card 5: "He must be at Joey's house. If he is there, I will give him an apple when he comes home."

Card 8 BM: "He always dreamed of being a doctor and wanted to help people a lot."

(b) *Mean, rejecting, punishing.* A character refuses to help or teach, neglects, rejects, hurts, punishes, or shows negative affect toward another character. If a child merits disciplinary action by the parent and is punished for a misdeed, do *not* score as punishing. Examples to be scored follow:

Card 2: "Her mother makes this man work real hard, because he hurt his—her mother's feelings."

Card 16: "This boy was always mean to other boys."

(c) *Unhappy, sad.* The story states that any character is sad, unhappy, discouraged, grief-stricken, depressed, crying, or weeping. For example:

Card 1: "Feels bad because he can't play."

Card 8 BM: "The boy is sad because the mother might die, and he doesn't want her to die."

Card 8BM: "That little boy and he looks sad."

(d) *Happy, glad.* The story states that any character is happy, glad, cheerful, thankful, laughing, and smiling. For example:

Card 1: "He took them and learned how to play. Then he was happy."

Card 8 BM: "Tom felt real good and thanked his father and the other man."

Card 16: "When I got home, I was happy that I had a fun time at the beach."

(e) *Aggression.* Hostile or threatening action by any character that causes fear or flight or brings the other person into forceful contact. Include acts of displaced aggression (e.g., the boy breaking the violin because he does not want to practice). For example:

Card 8 BM: "Then two crooks got him tied up."

Card 16: "...some bad man he tells him, 'Come on and have some candy.' Then the little boy go to ...and the guy grabs him and he is strangles him."

(f) *Dishonesty*. Instances of stealing, robbing, lying, cheating, or deception by any character. Abandonment of children should not be scored here. Examples for this item are:

Card 5: "She opens the door very quietly and she goes in to steal the money."

Card 8 BM: "He had no more friends because that he didn't have a hunting license. He had been hunting for so long and nobody noticed it."

Card 16: "So he said, 'If you help me, I'll pay you,' and the men said, 'All right.' Then when they were finished, he didn't pay them ... ."

(g) *Illness, injury*. Score instances in which any character is crippled, ill, sick, injured, in hospital, undergoing an operation, in poor health, or in an accident without reference to condition. For example:

Card 2: "She thought that her mother had a sickness that was going around and she was very painful looking."

Card 5: "So the others had a piece and they were poisoned."

Card 8 BM: "...this boy by the name of Tom was watching his father and another man—operate on—his friend."

Card 16: "She steps up to the side and tries to get the dog out of a fight. She gets hurt."

(h) *Death*. Score if any character dies, or may be presumed to be dying whether the cause of death is violent or nonviolent. If murder or killing is scored, death will also be scored. Examples follow:

Card 2: "...the letter had said that her mother had died, so her father came out to live with her ... ."

Card 16: "He didn't wake up the next morning. He's dead."

(i) *Murder, killing*. Score if any character murders or is murdered, kills or is killed, either intentionally or accidentally, or is in danger of dying as a result of violence. Do not score unless a death occurs or is occurring. (Unsuccessful attempts are scored under item 20e, Aggression.) Examples follow:

Card 8 BM: "He was asleep, and they cut him and killed him."

Card 8 BM: "Two men always took after him, and started killing everybody."

(j) *Parental protection*. Any indication of excessive parental protectiveness or overconcern for the child. Attributes include: trying to keep the child out of situations that might be unpleasant or embarrassing; is concerned about the possibility of the child getting hurt or becoming ill; protects from other children.

(k) *Parental casualness*. Attributes include: does not object to the child's loafing or daydreaming; lets the child do pretty much as he wants to; expects the child to have everyday disappointments; lets the child off easy when he does something wrong.

21. GOAL-ORIENTED BEHAVIOR. Goal-oriented behavior is defined as involving some expressed plan, intention, or action of one or more characters to attain a goal. It may generally be observed when the reaction of the character(s) to the environmental press determining the story theme takes the form of goal-oriented plans, intentions, or overt behavior. Such reactions are scored separately in respect to temporal aspects of goals accepted, whether the direction is toward or away from something, and status of outcome, in the subitems below.

The minimal type of action between the character and the environmental press is not scored as goal-oriented behavior. For example:

"The boy is looking at the violin" does not evidence such behavior. However,

"The boy is looking at the violin and thinking if he can play" is goal-oriented behavior since it involves a plan, intention, desire, or action.

Another example:

"The girl has books in her arms" is not scored, but

"The girl wants to go to school" should be scored.

(I) *Number indicated*

Where the elements of the theme are knit into a coherent major or principal theme, score 1. Do not attempt to break down such a theme into elements.

Where the story contains two or more different themes, as in the case where E interrupts and R elaborates a different theme, score 2.

In the case where R seems to change his mind and tells another theme, score 2.

(II) *Thematic goal behavior*

To determine the thematic goal behavior, for which temporal aspect, direction, and outcome are scored, first select the principal theme, which can be identified as:

(A) The theme involving the central character and the perceived environmental press.

(B) The interaction with the central character which seems to be most important to that character.

Then, score the principal theme for temporal aspect, direction, and status of outcome as follows:

(1) *Temporal aspect.* For each card, score 0 if no goal-oriented behavior as defined is present; score 1 if the goal is short range (today, this week, soon); score 2 if the goal is long range (years, "When I grow up").

(2) *Direction.* Consider the initial situation of the character in relation to the terminal situation:

(a) Score the following as "approach": 1

(i) The terminal situation is positive (save from drowning, prevents from being hurt, avoids pain).

(ii) The initial situation is positive with no threat of change to a negative situation.

(iii) The initial situation is negative and the terminal situation is positive.

(b) Score the following as "avoidance": 2

(i) The terminal situation is negative (the hero dies, is sent to jail, is spanked).

(ii) The initial situation is negative with no action taken to change it.

(iii) The initial situation changes from positive to a negative one.

(3) *Status of outcome.* Score 0 if the goal behavior has no outcome as defined by item 63 in the Structural Scoring Manual. A barrier is defined as a definite interference by another character or a natural catastrophe. Otherwise score as follows:

1. if the ending or outcome indicates that the purpose of goal behavior is satisfied and no barrier or obstacle prevented the attainment of the goal.

2. if the purpose of the goal behavior is satisfied despite a barrier or difficulty.

3. if goal attainment was prevented by an insuperable barrier or difficulty; failure.

4. if failure was the result of lack of capacity of the individual (physical, mental, social, financial, or other inability to cope).

5. if failure represents loss of interest, cessation of effort, or changed motive.

6. if the outcome depends upon conditions explicit in the story, i.e., "If he goes to school, he will become a doctor."

——○ ○ ○——

APPENDIX III

QUESTIONS FROM CYCLE II HEALTH EXAMINATION SURVEY FORMS USED IN THIS STUDY

CONFIDENTIAL — *The National Health Survey is authorized by Public Law 652 of the 84th Congress (70 Stat. 489; 42 U.S.C. 242c). All information which would permit identification of the individual will be held strictly confidential, will be used only by persons engaged in and for the purposes of the survey and will not be disclosed or released to others for any other purposes (22 FR 1687).*

FORM APPROVED
BUDGET BUREAU NO. 68-R620-54.6

DEPARTMENT OF
HEALTH, EDUCATION, AND WELFARE
PUBLIC HEALTH SERVICE
NATIONAL HEALTH SURVEY

HES-256

(1-5) _____

CHILD'S MEDICAL HISTORY - Parent

NAME OF CHILD (*Last, First, Middle*)	SEGMENT	SERIAL	COL. NO.
(6-11)			

NOTE: Please complete this form by checking the correct boxes and/or filling in the blanks where applicable.

When you have completed it, keep it until the representative of the Health Examination Survey calls on you within a few days. If there are some questions you do not understand, please complete the others and the person who comes for the form will help you with the ones that were unclear.

20. NOW TURNING TO THE PRESENT TIME, HOW WOULD YOU DESCRIBE THE CHILD'S HEALTH NOW?
1 ☐ Very good   2 ☐ Good   3 ☐ Fair   4 ☐ Poor
IF FAIR or POOR, what is the trouble? _____

21. IS THERE ANYTHING ABOUT HIS(HER) HEALTH THAT BOTHERS YOU OR WORRIES YOU NOW?
1 ☐ Yes   2 ☐ No
IF YES, what is the trouble? _____

28. HAS HE(SHE) EVER HAD ANY OTHER ACCIDENT OR INJURY THAT TROUBLED HIM QUITE A BIT?
1 ☐ Yes   2 ☐ No   3 ☐ Don't know

33. HAS THIS CHILD EVER HAD MEASLES?
1 ☐ Yes   2 ☐ No   3 ☐ Don't know
IF YES:
A. At what age? _____
B. Was he(she) sick longer than usual?
1 ☐ Yes   2 ☐ No   3 ☐ Don't know
C. Did he(she) have to go to the hospital?
1 ☐ Yes   2 ☐ No   3 ☐ Don't know
D. Did he(she) have a high fever for more than one week?
1 ☐ Yes   2 ☐ No   3 ☐ Don't know
E. Did he(she) seem to be unusually drowsy (sleepy) after the illness?
1 ☐ Yes   2 ☐ No   3 ☐ Don't know

35. HERE ARE SOME OTHER KINDS OF ILLNESSES OR CONDITIONS SOME CHILDREN HAVE. HAS YOUR CHILD EVER HAD:
A. Asthma?   1 ☐ Yes   2 ☐ No   3 ☐ Don't know
B. Hay fever?   1 ☐ Yes   2 ☐ No   3 ☐ Don't know
C. Any other kinds of allergies?   1 ☐ Yes   2 ☐ No   3 ☐ Don't know
D. Any trouble with his (her) kidneys?   1 ☐ Yes   2 ☐ No   3 ☐ Don't know
E. A heart murmur?   1 ☐ Yes   2 ☐ No   3 ☐ Don't know
F. Anything wrong with his(her) heart?   1 ☐ Yes   2 ☐ No   3 ☐ Don't know
G. A convulsion?   1 ☐ Yes   2 ☐ No   3 ☐ Don't know
H. A fit?   1 ☐ Yes   2 ☐ No   3 ☐ Don't know

50. IS THERE ANY PROBLEM WITH THE WAY HE(SHE) TALKS?
1 ☐ Yes   2 ☐ No   3 ☐ Don't know
IF YES, what is the problem?
1 ☐ Stammering or stuttering?   2 ☐ Lisping?   3 ☐ Hard to understand?

4 ☐ Something else? What is that? _____

PHS-T217-6
7/64

Form Approved
Budget Bureau No. 68-R620-S4.6

HES - 257

DEPARTMENT OF
HEALTH, EDUCATION, AND WELFARE
Public Health Service
National Health Survey

(1-5)_____

Child's Medical History - Interviewer

NAME OF CHILD (Last, First, Middle)	SEGMENT	SERIAL	COL. NO.
(6-11)			

5. Which **one** of the statements in each of these sets best discribes

_____ ?

a. (1) ☐ Eats too much (2) ☐ Usually eats enough (3) ☐ Doesn't eat enough

b. (1) ☐ Eats nearly all kinds of food

(2) ☐ Eats most kinds of foods, dislikes a few kinds

(3) ☐ Somewhat fussy about kinds of food he (she) eats

(4) ☐ Very fussy about food; won't eat many things

14. When it comes to meeting new children and making new friends is _____

☐ a. Somewhat shy   ☐ b. About average willingness

☐ c. Very outgoing - makes friends easily

15. How well would you say he gets along with other children?

☐ a. No difficulty; is well liked

☐ b. As well as most children

☐ c. Has difficulty with many children

17. Has anything ever happened that seemed to seriously upset or disturb your child?

☐ Yes   ☐ No

18. With respect to how relaxed or how tense or nervous your child is, would you rate him (her)

a. ☐ Rather high strung, tense and nervous.

b. ☐ Moderately tense.

c. ☐ Moderately relaxed.

d. ☐ Unusually calm and relaxed.

19. With respect to your child's temper or his (her) getting angry, would you rate him (her)

a. ☐ Has a very strong temper, loses it easily.

b. ☐ Occasionally shows a fairly strong temper.

c. ☐ Gets angry once in a while but does not have a particularly strong temper.

d. ☐ Hardly ever gets angry or shows any temper.

61

FORM APPROVED
BUDGET BUREAU NO. 68-R620-54.6

DEPARTMENT OF
HEALTH, EDUCATION, AND WELFARE
PUBLIC HEALTH SERVICE
National Center for Health Statistics
Health Examination Survey

HES-243

SUPPLEMENTAL INFORMATION FROM SCHOOL

The child whose name appears below is one of the sample of children being studied in the Health Examination Survey. Please complete this form on the basis of school records and/or information the child's teacher or other school official may have. Please return it in the enclosed franked envelope. This child's parent or guardian has given us written authorization to obtain information from the school.

School Number _____   Sample Child Number _____

Name of child: _____
                 (Last Name)   (First Name)   (Middle Name)

Home address (for identification)_____

4. Have any grades been repeated for any reason?   ☐ Yes ☐ No

8. If the following special resources were available, check those you would recommend for this child:

   a. ☐ Special provision for hard of hearing.

   b. ☐ Special provision for "sight saving".

   c. ☐ Speech therapy.

   d. ☐ Special provision for orthopedically handicapped.

   e. ☐ Special provision for gifted children.

   f. ☐ Special provision for "slow learners".

   g. ☐ Class for mentally retarded.

   h. ☐ Special provision for emotionally disturbed.

   i. ☐ Other (specify) _____.

   j. ☐ None of above.

11. Which one of these statements most accurately describes this child?

    ☐ A. His adjustment is at times a concern. You think of him as a problem or future problem.
    ☐ B. Unusual in his ability to cope with normal situations. At least occasionally have thought of him as "unusually well adjusted."
    ☐ C. You rarely think of him in terms of his behavior. He is not described by A or B.

12. As you know, the ability to pay attention to a task and to sustain attention (concentrate) changes with age, although children of the same age differ. Check the item which best describes the child in the classroom situation.

    ☐ A. Pays attention as well as most children his age.

    ☐ B. Characteristically is more attentive than others his age.

    ☐ C. Characteristically is less attentive than others his age.

    ☐ D. No basis for judging which of above fits this child.

13. In the classroom situation which one of these statements most nearly describes this child?

⬜ A. Almost constantly moving, inappropriately talks out loud, drops things, leaves his seat when he should not, finds reasons to be "on-the-move".

⬜ B. Slightly more restless than most children his age. But usually is not a problem in the classroom.

⬜ C. Shows average amount of restlessness if fatigued, bored, etc. Motor activity level is as expected for his age.

⬜ D. Remains quiet long after the average child has become restless. Sometimes seems too controlled for his age.

⬜ E. No basis for judging which of above fits this child.

14. Below are a list of statements which may or may not describe this child. If the statement is descriptive of him/her, place a check mark (✓) in front of the statement. If it does not describe this child, leave the space blank. (You may check several items).

⬜ A. Other children frequently accuse him of fighting.
⬜ B. "Accidentally" trips, shoves or hits other children. Is too "rough" with other children.
⬜ C. Frequently comes to your attention because he has been injured.
⬜ D. Agressive behavior frequently makes disciplinary action necessary.
⬜ E. Children frequently complain that he uses bad words.
⬜ F. Parents of other children call to complain about his behavior.
⬜ G. No method of discipline seems to work with him.
⬜ H. No basis for judging about this child in these areas.
⬜ I. None of above statements describe this child.

18. With respect to intellectual ability, would you judge this child to be:

⬜ A. About average for his age (neither in the top - about one-fourth, nor the bottom - about one-fourth)

⬜ B. Clearly above average for his/her age (In about the top fourth).

⬜ C. Clearly below average for his/her age (In about the bottom fourth).

⬜ D. No basis for judging this child.

19. With respect to academic performance, would you judge this child to be:

⬜ A. About average for his/her age (neither in the top - about one-fourth, nor the bottom -- about one-fourth).

⬜ B. Clearly above average for his/her age (In about the top fourth).

⬜ C. Clearly below average for his/her age (In about the bottom fourth).

⬜ D. No basis for judging this child.

——○ ○ ○——

CONVERSION TABLE AND PERCENTILE EQUIVALENT TABLE

Table VII. Conversions of raw scores on the 31 TAT variables to standard scores (t scores)

Item 1: Adverbs

Raw score	t score
0	45
1	47
2	49
3	52
4	54
5	57
6	59
7	61
8	64
9	66
10	69
11	71
12	73
13	76
14	78
15	81
16	83
17	85
18	88
19	90
20	93
21	95
22	97
23	100
24	102
25	105
26	107
27	109
28	112
29	114
30	117
31	119
32	121
33	124
34	126
35	129
36	131
37	133
38	136
39	138
40	141
41	143
42	145
43	148

Item 2: Pauses

Raw score	t score
0	41
1-2	42
3-4	43
5-6	44
7-8	45
9-10	46
11-12	48
13-14	49
15-16	50
17-18	51
19-20	52
21-22	53
23-24	55
25-26	56
27-28	57
29-30	58
31-32	59
33-34	60
35-36	61
37-38	63
39-40	64
41-42	65
43-44	66
45-46	67
47-48	68
49-50	69
51-52	71
53-54	72
55-56	73

Item 2: Pauses—Con.

Raw score	t score
57-58	74
59-60	75
61-62	76
63-64	77
65-66	79
67-68	80
69-70	81
71-72	82
73-74	83

Item 3: Verbatim repetitions

Raw score	t score
0	42
1	44
2	45
3	46
4	47
5	49
6	50
7	51
8	52
9	53
10	55
11	56
12	57
13	58
14	60
15	61
16	62
17	63
18	64
19	66
20	67
21	68
22	69
23	71
24	72
25	73
26	74
27	75
28	77
29	78
30	79
31	80
32	82
33	83
34	84
35	85
36	86
37	88
38	89
39	90

Item 4: Corrections

Raw score	t score
0	45
1	48
2	50
3	53
4	56
5	59
6	61
7	64
8	67
9	69
10	72
11	75
12	78
13	80
14	83
15	86
16	88
17	91

Item 4: Corrections—Con.

Raw score	t score
18	94
19	96
20	99
21	102
22	105
23	107
24	110
25	113
26	115
27	118
28	121
29	124
30	126
31	129
32	132
33	134
34	137
35	140
36	143
37	145
38	148
39	151
40	153
41	156
42	159
43	162
44	164
45	167
46	170

Item 5: Past reference

Raw score	t score
0	44
1	52
2	60
3	69
4	77
5	85

Item 6: Future reference

Raw score	t score
0	43
1	50
2	57
3	65
4	72
5	80

Item 7: Unhappy outcome

Raw score	t score
0	44
1	58
2	71
3	84
4	98
5	111

Item 8: Death

Raw score	t score
0	43
1	57
2	71
3	86
4	100

Item 9: Murder-killing

Raw score	t score
0	45
1	63
2	81
3	99
4	117

Item 10: Rejection

Raw score	t score
0	47
1	64
2	81
3	98
4	116
5	133

Item 11: Level of interpretation

Raw score	t score
0	3
1	7
2	11
3	15
4	19
5	23
6	27
7	31
8	35
9	39
10	43
11	47
12	52
13	56
14	60
15	64

Item 12: Situation complexity

Raw score	t score
0	4
1	8
2	13
3	17
4	21
5	25
6	29
7	33
8	37
9	41
10	45
11	49
12	53
13	57
14	62
15	66

Item 13: Present reference

Raw score	t score
0	-18
1	-3
2	10
3	24
4	39
5	53

Item 14: Happy outcome

Raw score	t score
0	45
1	59
2	73
3	87
4	101

Item 15: Causally connected statments

Raw score	t score
0	41
1	47
2	54

Item 15: Causally connected statements—Con.

Raw score	t score
3	61
4	68
5	75

Item 16: Expression of feeling

Raw score	t score
0	36
1	42
2	49
3	55
4	61
5	68

Item 17: Outcome

Raw score	t score
0	39
1	44
2	50
3	56
4	61
5	67

Item 18: Kind-loving

Raw score	t score
0	45
1	61
2	76
3	92
4	107
5	123

Item 19: Happy-glad

Raw score	t score
0	42
1	49
2	57
3	64
4	71
5	79

Item 20: Goal-oriented behavior

Raw score	t score
0	34
1	39
2	45
3	50
4	56
5	61
6	66
7	72
8	77
9	82
10	88

Item 21: Hostile antagonism

Raw score	t score
0	47
1	70
2	93
3	115
4	138
5	161

Item 22: Morbid mood

Raw score	t score
0	47
1	67

Item 22: Morbid mood—Con.

Raw score	t score
2	87
3	108
4	128
5	149
6	169

Item 23: Bizarre theme

Raw score	t score
0	39
1	45
2	51
3	57
4	63
5	69

Item 24: Egocentrism

Raw score	t score
0	45
1	64
2	83
3	103
4	122

Item 25: Mean, rejecting

Raw score	t score
0	45
1	59
2	74
3	88
4	103
5	117

Item 26: Aggression

Raw score	t score
0	42
1	56
2	69
3	83
4	96

Item 27: Possessive adjectives

Raw score	t score
0	42
1	43
2	44
3	45
4	46
5	47
6	48
7	50
8	51
9	52
10	53
11	54
12	55
13	57
14	58
15	59
16	60
17	61
18	62
19	63
20	65
21	66
22	67
23	68
24	69
25	70
26	72
27	73

Table VII. Conversions of raw scores on the 31 TAT variables to standard scores (t scores)—Con.

Raw score	t score	Raw score	t score	Raw score	t score	Raw score	t score	Raw score	t score
Item 27: Possessive adjectives—Con.		Item 28: Common nouns—Con.		Item 29: Pronouns—Con.		Item 29: Pronouns—Con.		Item 30: Single verbs—Con.	
28	74	87-90	60	18- 21	45	305-308	118	238-241	95
29	75	91-94	61	22- 25	46	309-312	119	242-245	96
30	76	95-98	62	26- 29	47	313-315	120	246-250	97
31	77	99-102	63	30- 33	48	316-319	121	251-254	98
32	78	103-106	64	34- 37	49	320-323	122	255-258	99
33	80	107-110	65	38- 41	50	324-327	123	259-262	100
34	81	111-114	66	42- 45	51	328-331	124	263-267	101
35	82	115-118	67	46- 49	52	332-335	125	268-271	102
36	83	119-122	68	50- 53	53	336-339	126	272-275	103
37	84	123-126	69	54- 56	54	340-343	127	276-279	104
38	85	127-130	70	57- 60	55	344-347	128	280-284	105
39	86	131-134	71	61- 64	56	348-351	129	285-288	106
40	88	135-138	72	65- 68	57	352-355	130	289-292	107
41	89	139-142	73	69- 72	58	356-359	131	293-296	108
42	90	143-146	74	73- 76	59			297-301	109
43	91	147-150	75	77- 80	60	Item 30: Single verbs		302-305	110
44	92	151-154	76	81- 84	61			306-309	111
45	93	155-158	77	85- 88	62	0- 3	39	310-313	112
46	95	159-162	78	89- 92	63	4- 7	40	314-318	113
47	96	163-166	79	93- 96	64	8- 12	41	319-322	114
48	97	167-170	80	97-100	65	13- 16	42	323-326	115
49	98	171-174	81	101-104	66	17- 20	43	327-330	116
50	99	175-178	82	105-107	67	21- 24	44	331-335	117
51	100	179-182	83	108-111	68	25- 29	45	336-339	118
52	101	183-186	84	112-115	69	30- 33	46	340-343	119
53	103	187-190	85	116-119	70	34- 37	47	344-347	120
54	104	191-194	86	120-123	71	38- 41	48	348-352	121
55	105	195-198	87	124-127	72	42- 46	49	353-356	122
56	106	199-202	88	128-131	73	47- 50	50	357-360	123
57	107	203-206	89	132-135	74	51- 54	51	361-364	124
58	108	207-210	90	136-139	75	55- 58	52	365-369	125
59	109	211-214	91	140-143	76	59- 63	53		
60	111	215-218	92	144-147	77	64- 67	54	Item 31: Dialogue	
61	112	219-222	93	148-151	78	68- 71	55		
62	113	223-226	94	152-155	79	72- 75	56	0	45
63	114	227-230	95	156-158	80	76- 80	57	1	47
64	115	231-234	96	159-162	81	81- 84	58	2	48
65	116	235-238	97	163-166	82	85- 88	59	3	50
66	118	239-242	98	167-170	83	89- 92	60	4	51
67	119	243-246	99	171-174	84	93- 97	61	5	53
68	120	247-250	100	175-178	85	98-101	62	6	54
69	121	251-254	101	179-182	86	102-105	63	7	56
70	122	255-258	102	183-186	87	106-109	64	8	57
71	123	259-262	103	187-190	88	110-114	65	9	59
72	124	263-266	104	191-194	89	115-118	66	10	60
73	126	267-270	105	195-198	90	119-122	67	11	62
74	127	271-274	106	199-202	91	123-126	68	12	63
75	128	275-278	107	203-206	92	127-131	69	13	64
		279-282	108	207-209	93	132-135	70	14	66
Item 28: Common nouns		283-286	109	210-213	94	136-139	71	15	67
		287-280	110	214-217	95	140-143	72	16	69
0- 2	38	291-294	111	218-221	96	144-148	73	17	70
3- 6	39	295-298	112	222-225	97	149-152	74	18	72
7-10	40	299-302	113	226-229	98	153-156	75	19	73
11-14	41	303-306	114	230-233	99	157-160	76	20	75
15-18	42	307-310	115	234-237	100	161-165	77		
19-22	43	311-314	116	238-241	101	166-169	78		
23-26	44	315-318	117	242-245	102	170-173	79		
27-30	45	319-321	118	246-249	103	174-177	80		
31-34	46	322-325	119	250-253	104	178-182	81		
35-38	47	326-329	120	254-257	105	183-186	82		
39-42	48	330-333	121	258-260	106	187-190	83		
43-46	49	334-337	122	261-264	107	191-194	84		
47-50	50	338-341	123	265-268	108	195-199	85		
51-54	51	342	124	269-272	109	200-203	86		
55-58	52			273-276	110	204-207	87		
59-62	53	Item 29: Pronouns		277-280	111	208-211	88		
63-66	54			281-284	112	212-216	89		
67-70	55	0- 2	40	285-288	113	217-220	90		
71-74	56	3- 5	41	289-292	114	221-224	91		
75-78	57	6- 9	42	293-296	115	225-228	92		
79-82	58	10-13	43	297-300	116	229-233	93		
83-86	59	14-17	44	301-304	117	234-237	94		

Table VIII. Percentile equivalents for TAT composite scores, by sex, age, and TAT factor

TAT factor and composite score	Boys						Girls					
	6 years	7 years	8 years	9 years	10 years	11 years	6 years	7 years	8 years	9 years	10 years	11 years
Factor I: Verbal productivity	Percentile											
245-255 ------------	0	0	0	0	0	0	0	0	0	0	0	0
256-260 ------------	18	11	12	3	4	2	21	14	10	7	1	4
261-265 ------------	44	31	26	16	16	10	43	34	21	17	5	11
266-270 ------------	65	48	39	28	23	17	52	51	36	24	15	15
271-275 ------------	72	59	47	37	31	25	65	60	41	33	22	23
276-280 ------------	83	68	56	44	40	30	71	66	53	46	32	28
281-285 ------------	88	73	58	52	46	36	74	70	61	49	37	38
286-290 ------------	89	77	66	55	56	43	79	74	65	54	42	41
291-295 ------------	92	80	68	61	60	46	83	79	69	55	46	45
296-300 ------------	93	84	73	67	64	51	86	80	72	60	51	59
301-305 ------------	93	87	79	70	67	54	88	80	78	63	55	63
306-310 ------------	95	88	80	74	70	58	88	82	80	66	58	68
311-315 ------------	96	89	81	80	74	61	88	83	80	67	62	73
316-320 ------------	96	90	84	83	79	68	93	84	84	71	63	77
321-325 ------------	96	93	88	85	82	70	93	86	86	72	64	80
326-330 ------------	96	93	88	85	84	74	93	89	88	77	68	82
331-335 ------------	97	95	91	88	85	75	94	90	91	79	71	84
336-340 ------------	97	95	93	91	85	76	95	91	91	82	78	85
341-345 ------------	97	95	93	91	87	77	95	92	92	83	81	85
346-350 ------------	97	95	94	91	90	78	98	92	92	83	83	87
351-355 ------------	97	96	94	94	91	82	98	94	94	83	84	88
356-360 ------------	97	96	95	94	91	82	98	95	94	85	85	90
361-365 ------------	97	96	95	95	91	84	98	95	94	86	86	91
366-370 ------------	97	97	97	95	92	87	98	97	94	89	86	91
371-375 ------------	97	97	97	95	93	88	98	97	95	89	88	91
376-380 ------------	97	97	97	96	94	89	98	97	95	90	88	93
381-385 ------------	98	97	97	96	95	91	98	97	95	91	92	93
386-390 ------------	98	98	97	98	95	92	98	97	95	91	94	93
391-395 ------------	98	98	97	98	96	92	98	98	95	91	95	96
396-400 ------------	98	98	97	98	96	92	99	99	95	92	96	96
401-405 ------------	98	98	97	98	96	93	99	100	96	92	97	97
406-410 ------------	98	98	97	99	96	93	99	100	96	93	97	97
411-415 ------------	99	98	97	99	96	93	99	100	97	93	98	97
416-420 ------------	99	99	98	99	97	95	99	100	97	93	98	97
421-425 ------------	99	99	99	99	98	95	99	100	97	94	98	97
426-430 ------------	100	99	99	99	98	96	99	100	98	95	99	97
431-435 ------------	100	99	99	99	98	96	99	100	98	95	99	97
436-440 ------------	100	99	99	99	98	98	99	100	98	97	99	97
441-445 ------------	100	99	99	99	100	98	99	100	98	97	99	97
446-450 ------------	100	99	99	99	100	98	99	100	98	97	99	97
451-455 ------------	100	99	99	99	100	98	99	100	98	98	99	97
456-460 ------------	100	99	99	99	100	98	100	100	98	99	99	97
461-465 ------------	100	99	99	99	100	98	100	100	99	99	99	97
466-470 ------------	100	100	100	100	100	100	100	100	100	100	100	100
Factor II: Dysphoric mood												
125 ----------------	0	0	0	0	0	0	0	0	0	0	0	0
126-130 ------------	58	63	53	54	52	47	54	55	52	59	45	47
131-135 ------------	58	63	53	54	52	47	54	55	52	59	45	47
136-140 ------------	58	63	53	54	52	47	54	55	52	59	45	47
141-145 ------------	67	77	63	68	64	63	73	68	67	75	62	67
146-150 ------------	68	77	64	68	65	63	73	68	67	75	62	67
151-155 ------------	69	78	64	70	69	64	73	72	68	75	64	70
156-160 ------------	70	79	65	76	72	74	73	76	73	77	72	74
161-165 ------------	86	86	82	85	83	80	86	86	86	85	75	79
166-170 ------------	87	86	85	87	83	83	86	89	87	87	78	84
171-175 ------------	90	92	88	94	90	90	93	92	92	93	84	88
176-180 ------------	90	92	88	94	90	90	93	92	92	93	84	88
181-185 ------------	90	94	90	95	91	91	95	93	93	93	86	90
186-190 ------------	91	96	94	96	93	93	98	95	96	95	93	94
191-195 ------------	93	96	95	97	95	93	98	95	97	95	94	97
196-200 ------------	93	96	95	97	95	94	98	95	97	95	95	97
201-205 ------------	93	99	98	97	96	96	98	95	97	98	98	98
206-210 ------------	95	100	99	99	97	99	98	97	98	98	98	98
211-215 ------------	96	100	99	100	97	99	98	97	98	98	98	98
216-220 ------------	98	100	99	100	98	100	99	97	98	98	99	99

Table VIII. Percentile equivalents for TAT composite scores, by sex, age, and TAT factor—Con.

TAT factor and composite score	Boys						Girls					
	6 years	7 years	8 years	9 years	10 years	11 years	6 years	7 years	8 years	9 years	10 years	11 years
Factor II: Dysphoric mood—Con.						Percentile						
221-225	98	100	99	100	99	100	99	97	98	98	99	99
226-230	98	100	100	100	99	100	99	97	99	98	99	99
231-235	98	100	100	100	99	100	99	99	99	99	99	99
236-240	99	100	100	100	99	100	99	100	99	99	99	99
241-245	99	100	100	100	99	100	99	100	99	99	99	99
246-250	99	100	100	100	99	100	99	100	99	99	99	99
251-255	99	100	100	100	99	100	99	100	99	99	100	99
256-260	100	100	100	100	99	100	99	100	100	99	100	99
261-265	100	100	100	100	100	100	100	100	100	99	100	99
266-270	100	100	100	100	100	100	100	100	100	100	100	99
271-350	100	100	100	100	100	100	100	100	100	100	100	100
Factor III: Conceptual maturity												
-75	1	0	1	1	0	0	4	0	2	1	0	0
-74 to -70	1	0	1	1	0	0	4	0	2	1	0	0
-69 to -65	1	0	1	1	0	0	4	0	2	1	0	0
-64 to -60	1	0	1	1	0	0	5	0	2	1	0	0
-59 to -55	1	0	1	1	0	0	5	0	2	1	0	0
-54 to -50	3	1	2	1	0	0	6	0	2	1	0	0
-49 to -45	4	1	2	1	0	0	7	0	2	1	0	0
-44 to -40	4	2	3	1	0	0	7	0	2	1	0	0
-39 to -35	4	2	3	1	0	0	7	0	2	1	0	0
-34 to -30	4	2	3	1	0	0	7	0	2	1	0	0
-29 to -25	4	2	3	1	0	0	7	0	2	1	0	0
-24 to -20	4	2	3	1	0	0	10	1	2	1	0	0
-19 to -15	4	2	3	1	0	0	10	1	2	2	0	0
-14 to -10	4	2	3	1	0	0	10	1	2	3	0	0
-9 to -5	4	2	3	1	0	0	10	1	2	3	0	0
-4 to 0	5	5	4	2	2	1	14	3	4	3	0	0
1-5	5	5	5	2	2	1	14	4	4	4	0	0
6-10	5	5	5	2	2	1	14	4	4	4	0	0
11-15	5	5	5	2	2	1	14	4	4	4	0	0
16-20	5	5	5	2	3	1	14	4	4	5	0	0
21-25	7	6	7	2	3	1	14	5	5	6	1	0
26-30	7	6	7	2	3	1	14	6	5	7	1	0
31-35	7	6	7	2	3	1	14	6	5	7	1	0
36-40	10	10	7	2	4	1	15	6	5	9	1	0
41-45	16	16	9	7	8	1	21	8	7	11	1	2
46-50	17	19	11	7	8	2	25	9	8	12	2	2
51-55	19	20	12	7	8	4	27	11	9	13	4	2
56-60	20	21	12	8	8	4	30	11	11	13	5	3
61-65	21	21	13	8	8	4	30	12	11	13	5	4
66-70	22	23	14	8	8	4	31	14	11	13	5	4
71-75	24	23	15	10	8	4	35	14	11	13	5	6
76-80	24	24	18	10	9	4	35	15	12	13	6	6
81-85	28	26	19	11	11	6	36	17	15	14	6	6
86-90	29	28	20	14	11	6	39	18	17	16	7	6
91-95	62	42	33	21	23	10	52	36	30	25	14	10
96-100	83	68	59	41	37	30	69	62	52	38	31	25
101-105	90	76	64	55	45	41	79	76	61	42	36	32
106-110	96	86	72	62	55	51	85	79	67	60	45	38
111-115	97	89	76	69	67	60	87	83	72	68	54	45
116-120	99	95	90	85	78	78	94	94	87	84	64	66
121-125	100	97	92	92	87	87	95	97	88	92	73	77
126-130	100	99	96	97	92	91	98	98	97	94	84	87
131-150	100	100	100	100	100	100	100	100	100	100	100	100
Factor IV: Narrative fluency												
275-280	0	0	0	0	0	0	0	0	0	0	0	0
281-285	20	10	5	1	4	2	15	8	6	5	0	0
286-290	31	21	14	8	9	2	25	18	9	8	0	1
291-295	43	26	24	13	11	4	36	23	13	11	1	4
296-300	55	32	32	19	14	7	40	29	21	13	3	7
301-305	63	35	36	21	16	9	48	36	26	15	7	7
306-310	69	40	43	24	18	10	54	42	30	19	9	8

Table VIII. Percentile equivalents for TAT composite scores, by sex, age, and TAT factor—Con.

TAT factor and composite score	Boys						Girls					
	6 years	7 years	8 years	9 years	10 years	11 years	6 years	7 years	8 years	9 years	10 years	11 years
Factor IV: Narrative fluency—Con.					Percentile							
311-315	72	48	47	28	23	14	58	48	35	21	14	11
316-320	80	57	53	30	32	19	61	59	39	28	18	13
321-325	85	62	55	33	35	23	63	64	47	30	20	21
326-330	87	68	57	40	36	28	67	67	52	31	22	23
331-335	90	74	59	43	41	29	68	69	57	34	28	26
336-340	92	77	63	46	44	30	69	69	58	37	28	26
341-345	93	80	67	52	47	35	73	73	61	42	35	28
346-350	94	81	68	58	49	41	76	76	66	45	35	35
351-355	97	83	69	64	54	45	77	80	68	49	38	36
356-360	97	85	74	66	60	50	81	81	71	51	39	39
361-365	97	86	74	70	61	54	87	82	73	54	43	45
366-370	98	88	77	72	65	58	87	85	77	58	47	47
371-375	98	90	86	74	68	63	87	86	79	63	51	51
376-380	98	92	87	77	71	69	88	89	80	65	54	56
381-385	98	93	88	79	72	69	88	91	82	68	57	58
386-390	98	93	89	83	75	70	90	94	82	69	58	60
391-395	98	93	91	84	78	76	90	96	84	71	63	63
396-400	98	94	91	86	79	80	92	96	84	77	69	64
401-405	98	95	91	87	80	81	92	96	86	81	72	65
406-410	98	95	92	88	83	84	92	96	87	82	75	69
411-415	99	95	93	88	86	88	92	96	88	82	77	70
416-420	100	95	94	89	90	89	94	96	89	83	78	75
421-425	100	96	94	93	91	91	95	97	89	83	79	76
426-430	100	97	95	94	93	91	96	97	90	83	81	80
431-435	100	98	97	94	94	92	99	99	90	84	82	84
436-440	100	98	97	95	95	95	99	99	92	87	85	84
441-445	100	98	97	96	96	97	99	99	93	91	86	86
446-450	100	98	97	98	97	99	100	99	95	93	89	88
451-455	100	98	98	98	98	99	100	100	95	93	91	89
456-460	100	98	98	99	98	99	100	100	96	93	92	89
461-465	100	98	98	100	98	99	100	100	97	94	92	91
466-470	100	98	98	100	98	99	100	100	97	96	93	92
471-475	100	98	98	100	98	99	100	100	97	98	94	93
476-480	100	98	98	100	98	99	100	100	97	99	98	93
481-485	100	99	100	100	99	99	100	100	97	99	99	95
486-490	100	99	100	100	99	100	100	100	98	99	99	96
491-495	100	99	100	100	99	100	100	100	98	100	99	97
496-500	100	100	100	100	100	100	100	100	100	100	100	100
Factor V: Emotionality												
265	0	0	0	0	0	0	0	0	0	0	0	0
266-270	44	42	39	35	36	25	50	45	35	30	35	44
271-275	44	42	39	35	36	25	50	45	35	30	35	44
276-280	44	42	39	35	36	25	50	45	35	30	35	44
281-285	67	66	59	60	56	47	69	66	55	58	51	59
286-290	71	68	63	66	61	55	70	70	57	62	53	64
291-295	73	70	67	67	64	58	73	71	62	68	56	65
296-300	85	74	73	70	70	64	79	76	66	74	62	70
301-305	86	79	82	76	73	67	87	82	77	79	69	75
306-310	86	82	85	78	74	68	87	83	77	80	73	76
311-315	87	83	86	81	76	69	87	83	79	82	74	76
316-320	90	88	88	86	80	73	90	85	87	85	78	81
321-325	90	90	88	86	83	74	90	91	89	86	79	84
326-330	91	92	88	86	85	77	90	92	91	88	83	84
331-335	91	95	89	87	91	85	92	93	92	89	86	85
336-340	92	95	90	88	93	87	83	95	92	92	87	85
341-345	94	95	91	88	94	88	93	96	93	93	87	89
346-350	95	95	91	88	94	89	93	96	95	95	88	90
351-355	96	96	93	88	96	90	93	96	95	96	91	90
356-360	98	96	93	90	96	91	95	97	96	97	93	91
361-365	98	97	93	92	96	92	95	97	97	97	93	92
366-370	99	98	93	95	96	93	96	98	97	97	93	93
371-375	99	98	93	95	96	95	98	99	97	97	94	93
376-380	99	98	94	97	96	95	98	99	97	98	94	93
381-385	99	99	95	98	96	97	99	99	97	98	94	93

Table VIII. Percentile equivalents for TAT composite scores, by sex, age, and TAT factor—Con.

TAT factor and composite score	Boys						Girls					
	6 years	7 years	8 years	9 years	10 years	11 years	6 years	7 years	8 years	9 years	10 years	11 years
Factor V: Emotionality—Con.	Percentile											
386-390	99	99	95	98	96	98	99	99	97	98	94	94
391-395	99	99	96	98	96	98	99	99	97	98	96	94
396-400	99	99	97	98	96	98	99	99	97	98	97	94
401-405	99	99	97	98	96	99	99	99	97	99	97	94
406-410	99	99	97	98	96	99	99	99	98	99	97	95
411-415	99	99	97	99	96	100	99	99	98	99	97	95
416-420	99	99	97	99	97	100	99	99	98	100	97	95
421-425	99	99	98	99	97	100	99	99	98	100	99	96
426-430	99	99	99	99	97	100	99	99	99	100	99	98
431-435	99	99	99	99	97	100	99	99	99	100	99	98
436-440	99	99	100	99	97	100	99	99	99	100	99	98
441-445	99	100	100	99	98	100	99	99	99	100	99	98
446-450	99	100	100	99	98	100	100	99	99	100	99	98
451-455	99	100	100	99	98	100	100	99	99	100	100	98
456-460	99	100	100	99	98	100	100	99	99	100	100	98
461-465	99	100	100	99	98	100	100	99	99	100	100	98
466-470	99	100	100	99	98	100	100	99	99	100	100	98
471-475	99	100	100	99	98	100	100	99	99	100	100	98
476-480	99	100	100	100	99	100	100	99	100	100	100	98
481-485	99	100	100	100	99	100	100	99	100	100	100	98
486-490	100	100	100	100	100	100	100	100	100	100	100	100
Factor VI: Verbal fluency												
195-200	0	0	0	0	0	0	0	0	0	0	0	0
201-205	8	1	3	2	1	1	13	3	4	2	0	0
206-210	26	13	14	7	5	1	26	10	9	8	1	2
211-215	44	32	30	12	16	11	46	23	15	12	3	6
216-220	64	42	39	25	28	16	57	37	25	20	11	8
221-225	78	57	46	35	32	22	65	51	41	29	20	18
226-230	88	65	55	45	39	30	74	58	48	37	27	24
231-235	90	74	59	52	45	37	79	70	56	39	33	33
236-240	93	75	65	61	53	47	82	75	67	49	40	39
241-245	95	79	71	65	64	54	83	80	70	53	46	45
246-250	95	82	75	69	67	57	85	84	75	59	51	52
251-255	96	85	79	74	71	59	86	89	77	64	55	57
256-260	97	86	81	75	73	63	86	90	80	68	59	62
261-265	97	87	84	80	76	67	87	90	82	74	63	66
266-270	97	90	85	82	77	70	87	93	83	75	66	72
271-275	97	91	88	86	80	76	87	93	83	76	69	77
276-280	97	91	89	89	83	79	87	93	84	80	71	80
281-285	97	93	89	89	85	81	89	94	85	84	74	82
286-290	98	95	90	90	86	82	93	95	85	87	76	84
291-295	99	95	92	91	86	82	94	97	87	87	77	85
296-300	99	95	92	91	90	85	94	97	87	87	80	86
301-305	99	95	92	94	91	88	95	98	89	88	81	86
306-310	99	97	92	94	92	88	95	99	90	90	83	86
311-315	99	97	94	94	92	90	95	99	91	92	84	86
316-320	99	97	94	94	93	91	98	99	92	92	85	87
321-325	99	97	95	94	95	92	98	99	92	94	86	88
326-330	100	97	95	94	95	93	98	99	92	94	87	90
331-335	100	97	96	94	96	95	99	99	94	94	88	91
336-340	100	98	97	94	96	95	99	100	94	95	89	92
341-345	100	98	97	96	96	95	99	100	95	95	91	92
346-350	100	99	97	98	97	95	100	100	95	96	91	92
351-355	100	99	98	98	97	95	100	100	96	96	92	93
356-360	100	100	98	98	98	95	100	100	96	97	95	93
361-365	100	100	98	98	98	95	100	100	96	98	95	94
366-370	100	100	98	98	98	95	100	100	96	99	96	95
371-375	100	100	98	98	98	96	100	100	96	99	96	95
376-380	100	100	98	98	98	96	100	100	96	99	96	95
381-385	100	100	98	98	98	96	100	100	96	99	96	96
386-390	100	100	98	98	99	96	100	100	96	99	96	96
391-395	100	100	98	98	99	97	100	100	96	99	96	96
396-400	100	100	99	99	99	97	100	100	96	99	96	96
401-405	100	100	99	99	99	97	100	100	96	99	96	97
406-410	100	100	99	99	99	97	100	100	96	99	97	97
411-415	100	100	99	99	99	99	100	100	97	99	97	97
416-420	100	100	100	100	100	100	100	100	100	100	100	100

—o o o—

APPENDIX V

WEIGHTS FOR THE 31 TAT VARIABLES ON THE SIX UNCORRELATED FACTORS

Table IX. Weights for the 31 TAT variables on the six uncorrelated factors

Variable	TAT factor					
	I	II	III	IV	V	VI
1. Adverbs	0.15	-0.02	-0.04	0.04	0.05	0.06
2. Pauses	0.24	-0.04	0.03	-0.14	-	-
3. Verbatim repetitions	0.13	-0.04	0.03	-0.15	-0.01	0.11
4. Corrections	0.31	-	-0.01	-0.13	-	-0.06
5. Past reference	0.27	-0.01	-0.04	0.02	-	-0.17
6. Future reference	0.27	-	-0.05	0.10	-	-0.23
7. Unhappy outcome	0.03	0.30	-0.07	0.20	0.03	-0.23
8. Death	-0.05	0.41	-0.01	-0.02	0.08	0.06
9. Murder-killing	-0.05	0.39	-	-0.08	0.03	0.08
10. Rejection	0.01	0.02	-0.41	0.12	-0.01	0.01
11. Level of interpretation	-0.08	0.03	0.19	0.11	0.04	-
12. Situation complexity	0.04	0.01	0.17	0.06	0.02	-0.05
13. Present reference	-0.01	-0.03	0.41	-0.11	0.01	-0.02
14. Happy outcome	-0.04	-0.05	-0.07	0.27	0.06	-0.02
15. Causally connected statements	-0.15	0.07	-0.04	0.21	0.05	0.09
16. Expression of feeling	-0.02	-0.01	-	0.18	-0.01	-0.05
17. Outcome	0.03	0.09	-0.08	0.31	0.06	-0.16
18. Kind-loving	-0.16	-0.13	-0.03	0.10	-0.14	0.12
19. Happy-glad	-0.04	-0.07	-0.06	0.13	0.03	0.07
20. Goal behavior	-0.07	-0.09	0.05	0.10	-0.22	-0.06
21. Antagonism	-0.02	-0.11	-0.06	0.03	-0.32	-0.05
22. Morbid mood quality	0.08	-0.11	0.03	-0.14	-0.20	-
23. Bizarre theme	-0.03	0.08	-0.01	-0.05	-0.26	-0.03
24. Egocentrism	0.11	-0.02	-0.03	0.02	-0.21	-0.17
25. Mean-rejecting	-0.03	-0.02	-0.05	0.02	-0.31	-0.05
26. Aggression	-0.01	0.05	0.06	-0.10	-0.27	-0.03
27. Possessive adjectives	-0.02	-	-0.03	-	0.03	0.22
28. Common nouns	-0.02	-	-	-0.06	0.03	0.26
29. Pronouns	-	-	-0.01	-0.02	0.02	0.21
30. Single verbs	-	-	-	-0.05	0.03	0.24
31. Dialogue	-0.10	0.02	-0.03	-0.05	0.05	0.32

———○○○———

☆ U. S. GOVERNMENT PRINTING OFFICE : 1974 543—881/49

VITAL AND HEALTH STATISTICS PUBLICATION SERIES

Originally Public Health Service Publication No. 1000

Series 1. Programs and collection procedures. — Reports which describe the general programs of the National Center for Health Statistics and its offices and divisions, data collection methods used, definitions, and other material necessary for understanding the data.

Series 2. Data evaluation and methods research. — Studies of new statistical methodology including: experimental tests of new survey methods, studies of vital statistics collection methods, new analytical techniques, objective evaluations of reliability of collected data, contributions to statistical theory.

Series 3. Analytical studies — Reports presenting analytical or interpretive studies based on vital and health statistics, carrying the analysis further than the expository types of reports in the other series.

Series 4. Documents and committee reports. — Final reports of major committees concerned with vital and health statistics, and documents such as recommended model vital registration laws and revised birth and death certificates.

Series 10. Data from the Health Interview Survey. — Statistics on illness, accidental injuries, disability, use of hospital, medical, dental, and other services, and other health-related topics, based on data collected in a continuing national household interview survey.

Series 11. Data from the Health Examination Survey. — Data from direct examination, testing, and measurement of national samples of the civilian, noninstitutional population provide the basis for two types of reports: (1) estimates of the medically defined prevalence of specific diseases in the United States and the distributions of the population with respect to physical, physiological, and psychological characteristics; and (2) analysis of relationships among the various measurements without reference to an explicit finite universe of persons.

Series 12. Data from the Institutional Population Surveys — Statistics relating to the health characteristics of persons in institutions, and their medical, nursing, and personal care received, based on national samples of establishments providing these services and samples of the residents or patients.

Series 13. Data from the Hospital Discharge Survey. — Statistics relating to discharged patients in short-stay hospitals, based on a sample of patient records in a national sample of hospitals.

Series 14. Data on health resources: manpower and facilities. — Statistics on the numbers, geographic distribution, and characteristics of health resources including physicians, dentists, nurses, other health occupations, hospitals, nursing homes, and outpatient facilities.

Series 20. Data on mortality. — Various statistics on mortality other than as included in regular annual or monthly reports — special analyses by cause of death, age, and other demographic variables, also geographic and time series analyses.

Series 21. Data on natality, marriage, and divorce. — Various statistics on natality, marriage, and divorce other than as included in regular annual or monthly reports — special analyses by demographic variables, also geographic and time series analyses, studies of fertility.

Series 22. Data from the National Natality and Mortality Surveys. — Statistics on characteristics of births and deaths not available from the vital records, based on sample surveys stemming from these records, including such topics as mortality by socioeconomic class, hospital experience in the last year of life, medical care during pregnancy, health insurance coverage, etc.

For a list of titles of reports published in these series, write to:

Office of Information
National Center for Health Statistics
Public Health Service, HRA
Rockville, Md. 20852